SALUTE !

UNCORKED

UNCRKED

MY JOURNEY

THROUGH

-the-

CRAZY WORLD

OF WINE

MARCO PASANELLA

CLARKSON POTTER/PUBLISHERS

New York

Copyright © 2012 by Marco Pasanella

All rights reserved.

Published in the United States by Clarkson Potter/Publishers, an imprint of the Crown Publishing Group, a division of Random House, Inc., New York.

www.crownpublishing.com

www.clarksonpotter.com

CLARKSON POTTER is a trademark and POTTER with colophon is a registered trademark of Random House, Inc.

Library of Congress Cataloging-in-Publication Data

Pasanella, Marco, 1962–
Uncorked : my journey through the crazy world of wine / Marco Pasanella.
p. cm.
1. Pasanella, Marco, 1962– 2. Wine and wine making—Anecdotes.   3. Wine industry—New York (State)—New York—Anecdotes.   4. Pasanella and Son, Vintners (Firm) 5. Merchants—New York (State)—New York—Biography.
I. Title.   II. Title: One man's journey through the crazy world of wine.
TP548.P289 2012
641.2'2—dc23   2011038459

ISBN 978–0–307–71984–3

eISBN 978–0–307–98560–6

Printed in the United States of America

Book and jacket design by Stephanie Huntwork
Interior photography: © Tetra Images/Getty Images *(cork)*
Jacket photography: © Henrik Bostrom/Flickr/Getty Images *(man)*;
© Stockbyte/Getty Images *(popping cork)*

10 9 8 7 6 5 4 3 2 1

First Edition

To my son, Luca—
look what your dad got you into

CONTENTS

prologue

THE
BIG SPILL

A THICK, *purplish ooze bubbled out of the bottom of the shipping container sitting on the dock at Port Elizabeth, New
Jersey. It looked just like the putrefying goo that seeps under
the locked doors of self-storage units in cable TV dramas, tip-
ping off the cops to the corpses.*

*At least that's what I pictured in 2009 as I learned that the
steel box filled with 7,800 bottles of my wine, the one on which
I had bet the farm, was stranded on the dock during Memorial
Day weekend. One hour at 200 degrees—the temperature of a
car seat after just sixty minutes in the sun—is all it would take
to obliterate five years of work, worry, debt, and sacrifice. I had
dumped a successful career, tripled our mortgage, stressed my
marriage, and maxed out our credit cards. Was it all going to be
for fifteen hundred gallons of grape-flavored sludge? What, I ag-
onized, was I going to find when I cracked open the first bottle?*

*This was not the joyous rebirth I had imagined a few years
before.*

chapter 1

PLOW

FOR CENTURIES, winemakers assumed that a good till reanimated the soil. To start afresh, they believed, you just needed to turn all the soil upside down. They dutifully hoed their vineyards twice a year: once at the end of the growing season and again just before spring. Plowing peaked during the 1980s as interest in wine boomed worldwide. If the traditional light turnover twice a year was good, the enthusiastic hoers believed, a deep cleansing every few months with a five-hundred-horsepower Disk Ripper tiller was better.

In recent years, partly as a result of the advent of natural winemaking, plowing has become more thoughtful. Some conscientious growers have turned away from machines, which can chop up the roots along with the weeds, and toward horse-drawn plows. Old-fashioned tilling, they believe, gives you more control, preventing damage while breaking up undesirable plants and encouraging the vines to grow deeper by gently loosening the surrounding earth. "Go slow," they intone. "Be careful."

Other winemakers favor planting over plowing. During the off-season, they grow cover crops such as peas, oats, and clover between the rows of vines to minimize soil erosion. "Don't churn up dust," the nurturers aver. "Sprinkle some seed."

Some die-hard naturalists eschew both sowing and digging. The less they touch the soil, the better.

THE FISH GUY VANISHED. My wife, Becky, and I had barely managed to scrape together the down payment on our waterfront wreck of a five-story industrial building in Lower Manhattan's old Fulton Fish Market. But without the rent from the fish guy we weren't going to be able to live there, much less make any improvements (windows would be nice), unless we found a new tenant to replace him on the ground floor. Months passed until we finally found the perfect one: an enthusiastic would-be wineshop owner willing to take over the space. The only problem was that *he was me.*

I can't say that I was actively unhappy with my career in design—just a little stuck. I had recently finished doing the interiors of the Maritime, a trendy boutique hotel in Chelsea, and a penthouse triplex in the Hotel des Artistes, a labor of love. I had written a decorating how-to book, *Living in Style Without Losing Your Mind.* I had designed and curated an exhibition on the next wave of product designers for the International Contemporary Furniture Fair. I had taught at Parsons the New School for Design for more than a decade. I was still writing my column for the *New York Times* occasionally. But I started to have rumblings.

"IT HAS TO BE THE BLUE GRANITE," proclaimed my client with the closetful of Manolo Blahniks and the kitchen lined with empty teak cabinets. "But you already had them cut the Calacatta," I reminded the woman who was already on the third renovation in just as many years. "We finalized that six weeks ago," I added, trying to mask my impatience.

"I know," the put-together blonde admitted sheepishly, and then cooed, "Darling, just tell them to take it back. They can sell it to someone else."

"And please," she added offhandedly, "make sure I get full credit. Thanks, love."

I looked at the two-foot stack of stone samples for the countertops at my feet, the piles of fabric swatches arrayed on my desk, the bulletin board with the inspirational magazine clippings. I surveyed it all and realized that I had had enough.

This type of design wasn't making lives better. It wasn't even making anyone's life prettier. This was going in circles.

I needed to break the cycle.

So I opened up the fifty-year-old Laubade armagnac that my mom had given me. I doused the desk, set it on fire, closed the door, and never looked back.

If only.

In reality, I did what people of my background do: I reached into the wine rack and whipped out the best bottle Becky and I had, a brunello riserva we had been given as a wedding present. The tannic red needed another five years before it would be ready to drink. "Screw it," I told myself, "I'm taking action." As I strained to sip my big glass of bitter red wine, I pondered. After a half an hour, the glass was empty. My mouth felt dry. Still no epiphany. But I knew I had to find a way off my upholstered hamster wheel.

Tibor Kalman, the late graphic designer and a friend, once told me that he tried never to do anything more than twice. The first time, he reasoned, you panicked, made mistakes, but also had the freshness and the passion to do it well. The second time, you could reduce the anxiety and the screwups but still be excited about the product. By the third time, however, Tibor contended, it all became too rote. The bumps were smoothed out, but so was the passion. Tibor, I should point out, was a little nuts. But his worldview resonated with me. I could design another hotel or more fancy apartments. But was more the answer?

I wanted a change but was not going to shave my head and move to Tibet. Instead, in the year I turned forty, I finally got married and bought a house. But I was still restless. I've never really had a career track as much as a career web, albeit always rooted in design. I've made furniture, licensed housewares, designed apartments, and written about architecture, though I never really felt as if I had left any of those jobs behind forever.

In Italy, where I spent summers and holidays growing up, this kind of vocational variation seemed to be no big deal. Carlo Mollino was as well-known for his chairs as for his buildings—as well as for his pornography. Massimo Vignelli ("If you can design one thing, you can design everything.") created the iconic 1972 New York City subway map, equally iconic dishes, and, no less important to me, the wine label for one of my favorite producers, Feudi San Gregorio. And I've always identified with multidisciplinary types. Not so much with the big geniuses such as Leonardo, but with Renaissance men writ small, such as David Byrne: art rock plus Latin music plus biking (an interest we share). Or my friend Douglas Riccardi, half hip Brooklynite, half Italian grandma: he makes his own pasta as well as his own driftwood furniture (and weaves the rush seats).

As a wine lover with many interests, it should come as no surprise that Thomas Jefferson, president/architect/botanist/inventor/writer/oenophile, is my god. But I was more wowed to learn through his diaries that as ambassador to France, Jefferson took several solo monthlong wine excursions to savor, learn, and experience. If I couldn't hope to match his many talents, at least I could aspire to his level of curiosity.

Wine, I soon discovered, is perfect for people who like to explore: history, biology, anthropology, geology, geography, even philosophy. The deeper you dig, the more you find. My friend Jan D'Amore discovered why grapes are so easy to grow at the resuscitated Odoardi winery in Calabria despite the locals' pessimism. Two thousand years ago, the Romans had tended vines on the very same site and had described a felicitous microclimate.

Chalky soil explains why that Sancerre is so minerally. Vines trimmed in a double-Guyot (flat-topped) probably are growing in Bordeaux.

No wonder wine attracts so many geeks—it's easy to get drawn in by the minutia. There are legions of statisticians and numbers-obsessed oenophiles who attempt to quantify an essentially unquantifiable experience by assigning it some standard measures and rational explanations. I see the temptation.

But I love the mysticism even more. How can, for example, the well-educated consulting winemaker to a number of Italy's top producers honestly tell me that one gram ($\frac{1}{28}$ of an ounce!)

of ground-up cow horn spread over twenty-two acres of vineyard led to worldwide recognition of his fledgling vineyard? Is he crazy? Or am I?

Wine, I also realized early on, appeals to people who like secrets. Whether it's hedge funders determined to be more inside than their peers or the people who like *The Da Vinci Code*, wine aficionados tend to like mystery. And wine seems to demand a special knowledge. But the truly devoted seek more: they want to be clued in to the stories behind the labels, like that illustrious Burgundy producer now being eclipsed by his wife's much younger lover whose rescue of a once-hallowed vineyard that had fallen into disrepair makes him the next superstar. Think Thomas Pynchon with a little Umberto Eco thrown in. It's a seductive brew of fact, legend, and gossip.

I started to dream that maybe I'd get to wander the countryside, inspecting old cellars and chatting with vignerons. I'd definitely get to taste a lot of wine. I'm so there. I think.

In San Francisco, there's a beautiful and eclectic store that sells motorcycle jackets and cheese, among an array of other perfectly selected merchandise. But I just can't get myself to buy dairy products from a clothing store. If I were really serious about opening a shop, and the idea was slowly dawning upon me, I'd have to make it special because of its approach, not because I also sold wheels of Brie and very attractive pots.

When the fish guy left in 2004, we renovated the second floor while we debated what to put on the first. The vision remained nebulous until one night in January 2005 at what seemed like an unremarkable press dinner promoting the new Conran store under the Fifty-ninth Street bridge, I was seated next to Julie Lasky, then editor in chief of *I.D.* magazine. Smart, a good listener, and a heavy pourer, Julie coaxed me to confess my vague idea for a store downstairs from my new home. She then promptly exacted a promise from me to write a story for *I.D.* about its development. Nursing a walloping headache the next day, I cursed my lack of discretion and thought, "Now what?"

I thought of Charles and Ray Eames's short film *Powers of Ten*, which starts on a picnic blanket and zooms in and out from that spot to provide startling perspectives on the everyday. I have spent much of my career at that picnic, designing napkins and dishes. Occasionally, with my work on interiors as well as a book, I've danced around a power of ten or two. But I've never really strayed far from the blanket.

Perhaps because I was also going to be a dad soon, I felt ready to leave my blankie behind. But instead of joining the rush to become a global name, I decided to zoom in. I had become more interested in connecting with the folks in my new neighborhood than in doing business with the shoppers at the mall.

I didn't see this new possible venture as a stretch so much as a reaffirmation of what design is supposed to be all about: making daily life a little better and, if I was lucky, elevating the mundane into ritual. I also hoped that by seeing design from another power of ten, I might become a better designer.

Don't think I was being humble. In the pantheon of cool jobs, furniture designer had replaced supermodel. But to me, being a shopkeeper with a corkscrew in my pocket, an apron around my waist, and a pencil behind my ear just seemed way cooler.

With an open bottle of Chianti in front of me, I started to imagine frequent scopa (an Italian card game similar to hearts) and grappa-tasting nights. You play cards. You drink. Maybe you snack on a little salami and a hunk of cheese. Sure, I wanted to sell cases of La Tâche to Wall Street fat cats, but I also wanted my neighbors and family to have a good time. I wanted a place that sold dozens of choices of wines under $10. I wanted it to offer great guidance. I wanted it to have a secret back room. I wanted it to be really well designed, a place my customers would want to show their friends. But I didn't want it Designed with gratuitous blobs, catchy themes, or ersatz wine cellars.

So there it was: I had a motive in an empty space and a career idling briskly in neutral. I had the interest and passion. And now I had a plan, which I'd announced to fifty thousand people in a magazine article that I wrote on a whim. I just needed that last push.

In the end, it wasn't just romance that convinced me. The neighborhood was changing quickly. Directly behind us, the entire block was being beautifully renovated into high-end apartments. Studying the local demographics, I quickly found out that our South Street Seaport zip code was growing tremendously and now had the highest per capita income in New York City, higher than Tribeca or the Upper East Side.

Better yet, these new residents would be seeking out services, including liquor stores. There was no wine store within half a mile of us, and the closest one was more of a hip-flask-and-Thunderbird kind of place. The nearest decent retailer was a mile and a half away—in Manhattan! That's quite a schlep if you're lugging a few bottles of Côtes du Rhône.

And so Becky and I leaped.

WE HAD BEEN LOOKING for a building to buy for four years. Like many New Yorkers, Becky and I were always window-shopping for the next great place to live. We loved pointing to some un-renovated garret and imagining "how amazing would it be to live there!" Most of the ogling was pure fantasy, but the game was fun.

My dream had been to fix up a diamond in the rough, rent out a few apartments, and keep one space for Becky and myself. We had come close on some potential projects: a parking garage in what is now the center of New York's Chelsea art district, a Chinese social club on the Lower East Side facing Hamilton Fish Park. The one I kick myself about was a former male porno theater complete with turnstiles and facing the Hudson River—for $400,000. At the time, the waterfront location was forbidding and the place needed more cash for construction than I thought I could muster. The now seven-story building stands one block from the Richard Meier towers on Perry Street, where Martha Stewart's daughter has a triplex.

Enough looking already, I thought. Commit!

When a friend told me about a building he had bought in the Seaport, I decided to check out the low-profile neighborhood, and I noticed a sign hanging in front of a waterfront shell of a building. I was in love.

When we first bought our building on South Street in 2002, it was still part of the Fulton Fish Market. Every night, several hundred guys in big rubber boots with ice hooks slung over their shoulders, with names like Beansie and Tony Ice, would arrive. We'd hear the sound of fish-laden skids scraping along the asphalt as the forklifts shoved the day's cargo into place. Then the floodlit streets would become packed with sparkling fish laid out in the middle of the road. In the winter, there were bonfires in garbage cans, leaving the air thick with the smell of the East River, wood smoke, and fish. From our ramshackle fifth-floor loft, we'd watch these scenes unfold, occasionally leaning out on the fire escape to get a better glimpse of a particularly large fish or a noisy dispute. Living there felt like being an extra in a movie about nineteenth-century New York.

We'd been able to afford the graffiti-streaked hulk less than a year after 9/11 because it was a few blocks from Ground Zero. "A whole building for the price of a two-bedroom apartment," the broker gushed. The inspector we hired to survey it was a little less impressed. "Thank God you're young," he said. The in-laws from Pennsylvania asked, "You want our only daughter to live *here?*"

Our first step in 2003 was to buy out the top floor tenant, the web designer. With our now empty bank account, we renovated the space enough to make it habitable, removing the frosted glass that blocked the Brooklyn Bridge views and the two-story storage island that dominated the space.

Situated on one of the few remaining stretches of Manhattan's commercial waterfront, the warehouse may have been decrepit, but it also had sixteen windows facing the Brooklyn Bridge. The previous owner, a retired fishmonger, was eager to get rid of the crumbling wreck. Under all the soot, we saw a potentially stunning Federal-style waterfront home with tenants to help defray its operating costs. At least that was the plan. Three years before we decided to open up the wineshop, the ground floor was stacked with salmon instead of Brunellos and Barbarescos. Every day, Crescent City Seafood, which occupied the space at the time, used forklifts and wooden hand trucks to move in and out seventy thousand pounds of sashimi-grade sockeye. Crescent specialized in what the trade called "Jewish" fish (pike, whitefish, and salmon); the rest of my block between Peck Slip and Beekman Street was Italian. They sold just about everything else that swam, plus calamari. Perhaps that was why my fellow paisans seemed to welcome me so warmly.

Carmine, one of my favorite fishmongers, operated a few doors down. He liked to greet me in his cardigan and glasses, holding both of my hands in his and telling me that just seeing me made his day. "You're doin' good, kid." Carmine seemed to be just as charitable to everyone else except to someone he referred to as "that fuck Giuliani." In the 1980s, Carmine had additional business interests in the form of an informal parking concession that he "owned" under the FDR, the elevated highway that runs along the river on the east side of Manhattan. According to Carmine, Giuliani, then the district attorney and keen on making more of a name for himself, came to the Fulton Street Market one day to announce his intention to clean up the joint. When his visit was met with a squid tossed in his direction by what Carmine termed some "punk," Giuliani responded with a witch hunt, asking the fish guys to rat out the kid who did it. After they refused ("We take care of our own," Carmine reminded me), "the market," he said, "was wrecked. And just over a scungil."

Still, I could never quite think of this kind old man as a gangster, even if he would never speak to me on the phone—Carmine preferred to walk and talk—and was driven around in a Buick by a thuggy-looking kid. My wife was a little more suspicious when Carmine suggested that we open a Laundromat in his building after the market moved. "Launder?" Becky squealed. "Carmine's not interested in dry cleaning; he's talking code!" But I still can hear him: "Four bucks to iron a pair of pants? Now that's a racket!"

No one on the block has been better friends to me than the Fogliano brothers, who operated Fair Fish in the adjacent eighteenth-century buildings. Vinnie and Frank saw me bring my newborn son home from the hospital, and they always made sure we had seven fishes on Christmas Eve (even if we only had six people for dinner). Rugged in his denim shirt and mustache, Vinnie was the front man. Frank, whose soft hands stood in stark contrast to the cracked and weathered mitts of his fellow fish-mongers, dressed nattily in calfskin jackets; he preferred the rela-tive quiet of his second-floor office.

On raw January mornings, when I walked our dog, Guenda-lina, I'd see Vinnie surrounded by crates of fish, piles of slush, and dozens of helpers hefting carcasses with gaffing hooks, with his arms crossed, standing in front of his building calmly surveying the market chaos.

The Foglianos, like many vineyard owners, are consumed by what they do. What does a great producer do on his off time? Eat and drink wine. What does Vinnie do? Go fishing. As any-one who has ever seen *Deadliest Catch* or *Sideways* knows, there are many easier ways to make money. They forge on, but funda-mentally, both winemaker and fishmonger operate at the whim of nature. Good crop/good catch and they are happy. Bad crop/ bad catch and they both seem to get superstitious. At least from the viewpoint of this city boy, the noble farmer surveying his vines and the gritty seaman scanning the horizon at sunrise (al-beit under the shadow of the FDR Drive overpass) are equally romantic. The fish may now arrive in aircraft containers and the winery may look like an operating theater, but fishmonger and winemaker are still Old World. This may explain at least a little about how natural the transition from fish storage to wine store seemed to me, despite how it flummoxed my friends.

Harder to relate to were the equally crusty older artists and wannabes who settled in the area during the 1970s. Many of them took pride, like my former residential tenants who lived above the fish market, in having homesteaded in a scruffy neighborhood. "Heat, who cared about heat?" the web designer cum video maker who lived on the fifth floor told me. "We didn't even have stairs." A few were also bitter that somehow they'd not been plucked from that salty goop and sent on to painting superstardom.

What both subcultures shared was fierce loyalty to an area that, as far as both groups were concerned, no one else really knew about. To an extent, they were right. The Seaport Historic District, despite being three blocks from Wall Street, directly across the island from the World Trade Center, and a block and a half north of the Seaport Mall, was sub rosa. So central yet so small, it's easily overlooked. Among the ten million people who flock to the Seaport each year, just a few hundred, most of them Europeans, take the time to investigate the neighborhood. To New Yorkers, and I was among them, the sixteen-square-block grid south of the Brooklyn Bridge is practically invisible. Before we bought our building, I had last visited the Seaport area on a fourth-grade field trip to see the tall ships.

No one I met in this neighborhood—other than Carmine, who liked to wash down his calamari with a glass of Frascati—

seemed to care about wine. Consequently, it's unlikely I would have even entered the wine business if not for the untimely demise of our tenant, Crescent Fish, who never made it to that new market in the Bronx. In the insular world of fish, their downfall was variously attributed to (1) gambling, (2) alcohol [not wine, I suspect], (3) a Mexican snapper farm that went belly up. I suspect all three.

But the clearest evidence of something not quite kosher among the whitefish specialists was their office on the second floor of our building. The front space was unremarkable in its cruddiness. Behind the barred windows and beneath the buzz of the fluorescent tubes ruled the big-haired office manager (imagine *Working Girl* plus twenty years, minus the Melanie Griffith looks), whose main job seemed to be strewing handwritten fish orders over the peeling, vinyl-tiled floor.

Wander into the back room that my wife and I called the clubhouse and the mayhem was more obvious. The central feature was a scarred wood table littered with change and stabbed in the middle by a large knife. Adorning the walls were *Playboy* pinups studded with question-mark-shaped ice hooks impaled into the drywall. Among the weapons, the money, and the dice, I'm not sure exactly what they did up there, but I'm pretty certain they weren't playing bridge and drinking tea. On the windows, there was chicken wire in lieu of glass, and the bathroom, whose drain had been disconnected some years earlier, was in continuous use. There were piles of rubber boots caked in fish scales. To the side, there was also a door to a locked room that no one would enter and to which I was never given the keys.

The whole *Gangs of New York* scene was presided over by a

menacing guy with a buff body, bulging eyes, an explosive temper, and an ever-present gaffing hook slung over his shoulder. Some mornings, we could even hear his screaming four stories above the din of dozens of forklifts and delivery trucks. Once, the day after one of those fits, I noticed that one of his loaders had a black eye. Then they were gone. No big-haired office manager. No muscle-bound enforcer. No stacks of swordfish. Not even a scale. The space was empty. For a minute we panicked, but then we quickly adjusted to the absence of all that hubbub and the attendant fish odors. Now we just had to figure out how to fill the void.

When we first bought the five-story building, we had four tenants: the fish guys on the bottom two floors and three rent-stabilized tenants on the floors above. In New York City, rent-stabilized apartments are protected from sharp increases in rent, and tenants have the right to renew their leases indefinitely. If the graffiti, fish guts, and crumbling masonry were not enough to dissuade potential buyers, the prospect of permanent tenants locked into below-market rents would have turned off most rational buyers.

I HAD NO INTENTION of opening a wineshop. I dreamed of Sloppy Louie, proprietor of the eponymous fish restaurant immortalized by *New Yorker* writer Joseph Mitchell in *Up in the Old Hotel*. Louie, whose real name was Louis Morino, was a fisherman from Genoa who prepared fish so simply and so well that the fishmongers would bring him their catch to cook. Louie's had long tables and tin ceilings and was located smack in the center of New York's mercantile center (and a block from my building). Mitchell describes it as the kind of place where you might find a Schermerhorn (a family that first arrived in the city when it was called Nieuw Amsterdam) sitting next to a fisherman down the counter from a mobster. What they all craved was fresh fish done right, along with a heavy dose of authentic seaside ambience. Louie was, Mitchell explains, a crusty but consummate host, kind of the Sirio Maccioni of his day, albeit down-market and fifty years earlier.

During the 1930s, Louie's restaurant opened at five o'clock in the morning. Breakfasts, according to Mitchell, included kippered herring and scrambled eggs, shad roe omelets, and split sea scallops and bacon. Variety was also one of Louie's trademarks. Mitchell describes one day's menu as offering "cod cheeks, salmon cheeks, cod tongues, sturgeon liver, blue-shark steak, tuna steak, squid stew, and five kinds of roe—shad roe, cod roe, mackerel roe, herring roe, and yellow pike roe." And that was in addition to the standard seafood staples.

Having designed restaurants for some very savvy clients, I knew enough to not run one myself. But I imagined Mario Batali would make the perfect proprietor of an updated version of this classic Italian fish place. So I worked my connections, polished my pitch—and never made it past his assistant. Undeterred, I next approached Mary Redding, the owner of the West Village icon Mary's Fish Camp. Mary, along with her ex, Rebecca Charles, seemed to have single-handedly invented the haute lobster roll. With such a deft touch with local seafood, I thought Mary would be a natural. "Already committed to something else" read her seemingly truthful handwritten brush-off.

SLOPPY LOUIE'S CATFISH SAUTÉ

SERVES 2

Sloppy Louie's was a famed seafood restaurant originally situated a few doors down from our building. According to New Yorker *magazine writer Joseph Mitchell, Louie prepared fish so simply and so well that the fishmongers brought him their catch to cook.*

2 TABLESPOONS OLIVE OIL

2 POUNDS CATFISH FILLETS

FLOUR, FOR DUSTING

2 EGGS, BEATEN

4 TABLESPOONS BUTTER, MELTED

2 TABLESPOONS DRY SHERRY WINE

2 LEMONS, ONE FOR JUICE AND THE OTHER SLICED IN WEDGES FOR GARNISH

SALT AND PEPPER TO TASTE

1 TABLESPOON PARSLEY, CHOPPED

PAPRIKA

Heat 2 tablespoons of oil in a medium skillet until it's very hot. Lightly dust the catfish fillets with flour, then dip them in the beaten eggs. Fry the fish for about one minute on each side, just until pale gold. Pour off the oil. Add the butter, sherry, and lemon juice. Sauté the fish three more minutes per side, basting with the pan juices. Add salt and pepper to the sizzling fillets, if desired. Transfer the fish to a platter and garnish with parsley, lemon slices, and paprika.

So I put that fish restaurant idea on the back burner and listed the ground floor space with a broker. The market, I thought, would let me know what should be there. And it did. "Awesome," said the club entrepreneur upon opening the rear freezer early one morning as I tried to ignore his alcohol breath. Over the gurgle of his motorcycle, which he left idling on my sidewalk, an inner voice whispered, "Run!"

There were some attractive offers (the Bao Noodles outpost, the man from Piedmont who ended up opening a place around the corner), but the more these guys trudged through the coolers, the more uncomfortable I felt. Were they really going to make the space look good? Was it going to be too loud for us to live upstairs? In a city where the average restaurant lasts eighteen months, would they last? Or would their true legacy be a permanent rodent problem? And, perhaps surprising for someone who had lived over a fish vendor, what about the kitchen smells?

Meanwhile, Becky and I worried about the mortgage and carped about all the services missing in our transitional neighborhood. As excited as we both were about being nestled in the heart of the oldest part of New York City, with jaw-dropping views of the Brooklyn Bridge, we had no dry cleaner and couldn't find a good supermarket. We couldn't even find a decent bottle of wine!

And then (cue music) it clicked. Wineshops are clean, quiet, and genteel. You don't hear about liquor stores going out of business. And we both love wine.

Researching the history of our building, I also found that this wasn't the first time wine was sold on the premises. The struc-

ture, built in 1839, originally had been a pair of Federal-style
row houses commissioned by the boat outfitters Slate, Gardiner
and Howell, which supplied ships moored at the piers across the
street. In 1882, the enterprising Jim Flynn joined the two buildings and converted them into a tavern under a rooming house
(read: brothel). It was another fifty years before the girls were
replaced with fish.

I turned to one of the most venerated names in wine selling
in the metropolitan area and the only retailer in New York State
that seemed to have figured out how to work around local liquor
laws that prohibit the same owner from operating at more than
one location: Morrell & Company.

Morrell's, started during the 1920s by two resourceful brothers, Samuel and Joseph, initially sold Virginian wine of question-
able quality. Then, during Prohibition, they turned to supplying
churches and other houses of worship with sacramental wines, as
well as physicians, who could prescribe alcoholic beverages for
medicinal purposes. One of Morrell's most popular offerings was
a wine "tonic" called Virginia Dare that was made from the scup-
pernong grape, a little-known varietal grown extensively in that
state since the Colonial era.

In the 1950s, Sam's daughter, Charlotte, made the store more
up-market and frequently made trips to France to buy Bordeaux
and Burgundy. Business flourished, and Morrell soon established
itself as one of the country's premier sources of those coveted
producers. In 1994, Morrell's became the first New York retailer
to get into the lucrative and prestigious auction business.

Now run by Peter, Charlotte's son and a legendary New York
wine figure, and his sister, Roberta, Morrell's is one of America's

best-known names in wine. Along with Sherry-Lehmann and Acker Merrall & Condit, Morrell's is considered part of the trinity of New York's carriage-trade vintners.

Morrell's has an impressive store in Rockefeller Center. Next door, they recently put in a bustling wine bar, and they've opened locations on the Upper East Side and in East Hampton.

The man behind this expansion was Nikos Antonakeas, the dashing Greek husband of Peter's sister, Roberta. We met, we talked, and we drank. But we never really got past the dating stage. Nikos was intrigued but concerned about the lack of foot traffic. After digging a little deeper, I too became uneasy.

Nikos, I discovered, met the thirty-years-his-senior Roberta (age seventy-six) through her son, Jon, who in turn had met him on a street corner in Athens. While on vacation, Jon was looking for an antique necklace for his mother, and Nikos helped him find one. A year later, Nikos came to New York and looked up the name on the business card Jon had handed him. The two young men and Jon's mother had lunch together. Roberta offered the handsome Nikos a job on the spot. A year later, they married. But their partnership didn't seem built only on a mutual love of wine. Nikos was passionate, but according to one of his East Hampton colleagues, he also had a fiery temper. "Just make sure you get everything written down," he explained. More unsettling than Nikos's outbursts was the fact that the Morrell's flagship store, I later found out, was suffering. Staff turnover was high. The rent was staggering, and their prices were even more out of reach, a good 15 percent more than those of their competitors.

I then turned to a more trusted source, a firm older than even the incorporation of Manhattan. Berry Bros. & Rudd, founded in 1698 by the Widow Bourne, is London's oldest and most venerable wine and spirits purveyor. It still occupies the same Tudor building at 3 St. James's Street, has two Royal Warrants (this identifies them as officially recognized suppliers to the royal family), and a two-and-a-half-million-bottle inventory, including some of the world's most coveted wines in the rarest vintages.

Inside this extraordinary wineshop, with an incongruous coffee mill sign hanging out front, there are rich oak-paneled walls, burnished oval tables, elegant Windsor chairs, richly carved fireplaces topped with ornate heraldry. There's no wine on the shelves or anywhere in sight. Bottles traditionally were stored in the cellars, which stretch from St. James's Street to Pall Mall. It took Berrys' 303 years after the original store opened to offer self-service.

But under all those groined vaults, this august London store has long been startlingly innovative. Berrys' started as a coffee shop (hence the sign) whose marketing genius was to weigh customers—William Pitt, Beau Brummell, Lord Byron, and the Aga Khan among them—on an enormous coffee scale, a novelty in the days before mass production.

In the 1830s, as tea and coffee started to wane in popularity among London's elite, Berrys' briefly turned to beer, becoming the agent for Bass and Co.'s East India Pale Ale. Then, as anti-alcohol (and particularly anti-gin) sentiment grew, they moved to clarets, ports, and sherries, which, as the domain of the British elite, were left alone.

In 1903, during King Edward VII's reign, the royal doctor approached the Berrys for something to ward off the chill felt by His Majesty when in his "horseless carriage." Henry Berry sent over the firm's brandy and ginger cordial, originally known as "Ginger Brandy—Special Liqueur." More than a hundred years later, "The King's Ginger Liqueur," as it was subsequently renamed, continues to be a bestseller.

Their biggest breakthrough, however, was in 1923. Francis Berry created a light-colored whiskey blend that contrasted sharply with the dark, oily Scotches fashionable at the time. That delicate blend, named Cutty Sark after the famed clipper whose Scottish name was taken from a Robert Burns poem, "Tam O'Shanter," took off. By the 1960s, Cutty Sark, the "abbreviated chemise of a winsome wench" in Gaelic, dominated the US market. It's now sold in more than a hundred countries, and those mammoth sales have provided much of the capital for innovative expansion.

Berry Bros. & Rudd, among the first to recognize the importance of e-commerce, launched its website in 1994, a year before Amazon. In the intervening years, Berry also launched two wine schools as well as shops in Dublin, Hong Kong, and Japan.

Wouldn't Berry Bros. & Rudd be interested in opening up three blocks from Wall Street? Think of the splash they could make: the oldest London shop now in the oldest New York neighborhood at the epicenter of commerce. Wouldn't the historically entrepreneurial retailer want to seize a humongous new opportunity? Wouldn't the preeminent seller of high-end French wines want to be close to all those bulging pockets and hungry egos?

Nope. Or, as I recall, a more particularly British rebuff, the obsequious fuck off: "So kind of you to offer. So sorry we are not in position to act on this wonderful opportunity. Do let us know when you open. Best of luck."

Nothing like a little rejection to galvanize me. With Berrys' out of the picture, I knew two things: a wineshop would be ideal in that space, but finding the right one might take forever. And wasn't I the wine lover with the vision? The guy who was ready to take on a new challenge? Did it really matter that I didn't know anything about running a retail store? That I didn't have a clue about the wine business?

Well, yes, it did. But I was committed. And the adventure already had started.

chapter 2

PRUNE

PRUNING CAN SEEM SAVAGE to the uninitiated. While the soil is still muddy from winter storms, vineyard workers slash off the previous year's growth, reducing the vines to nubs.

Despite the violence, pruning is, at its heart, a delicate art. Overly zealous trims will stunt crops; timid clips will allow an unchecked explosion of low-quality grapes. Good cutting encourages better fruit, helps prevent diseases, and eases the harvest.

The pruner must always think ahead to the following crop as, often, only year-old canes are allowed to bear fruit. Some vines are trained to climb, some to crouch, others to bend up and down.

For all its savagery, pruning is about coaxing the best out of a malleable vine. The sharp cuts are about making choices with confidence; those irrevocable nips are about envisioning the future. In the end, with just a few stumps remaining on a gnarled stalk, pruning is about optimism. You just know it's going to grow.

ITH THE DREAM CRYSTALLIZED (and Becky pregnant), it was time, in early 2005, to focus on the pragmatic—as in how in the hell we were going to pay for this reverie. I did what every other red-blooded American appeared to be doing at the time: I doubled our mortgage. Actually, I increased it two and a half–fold. I tried not to dwell on why the only financial institution willing to finance our dream was an offshore bank on the fifth floor of a nondescript downtown office building. We were in deep, but we felt flush.

And flush was exactly what we needed. After its hasty departure the previous year, our fish tenant had left us a smelly box with concrete floors punctured by floor drains clogged with fish scales. There was no heat. There weren't even doors and windows behind the rusty roll-down gates. During these early days, I spent a lot of time wandering around the various crannies muttering, "Shit," as I discovered one wrinkle after another: the compressor is leaking Freon. "Shit." The electrical cords are mounted with duct tape. "Shit." The peeling paint looks old enough to contain lead. "Shit, shit!"

Once the space was cleared, the real challenge became clear: What was this store going to look like? Most wineshops are organized geographically (e.g., Italian in aisle 1 and French in aisle 2). Fancy liquor and hip flasks, the items most likely to be shoplifted, are displayed behind the counter. As in grocery stores, the layout tends to be "racetrack": The customer is led in a large oval, or "power aisle," that features a main thoroughfare sprouting minor branches. Aisles typically are separated with gondolas, the ubiquitous double-sided display racks best suited for show-ing off boxes of Lucky Charms. Shelf talkers, invariably rave de-scriptions of every choice, are tacked below the bottles. Bigger stores often use the preprinted ones from their wine distributors. Stacked on the floor near the entry is the inventory you hope to move. Either it has the best markup (wineshops make more on the cheap stuff) or it is the junk you were forced into buying to get something of higher quality that you wanted.

In Europe, a hands-off approach still dominates. Stores typi-cally display one bottle of each selection, often behind closed cabinet doors. You must ask for help if you actually want to hold a bottle. New York's Sherry-Lehmann recently renovated its flagship, using a similar model. Display bottles are under lock and key, and stock is sent up from the basement by notifying a clerk. Buying wine feels luxurious—and intimidating. Neither of these directions was particularly compelling to us.

My brother Nicolas was also one of those naysayers. "Who's really going to buy wine down in that godforsaken neighbor-hood?" my skeptical sibling asked me. "Malt liquor, maybe," he offered, "but *wine*?"

Nicky's doubts juiced my enthusiasm. Despite being whip-smart (he's an architect and successful real estate developer), my brother is staggeringly trend-deaf. When Starbucks was opening its first New York store, I remember his dismissal: "Cappuccino?" he scoffed, "Who's going to pay four bucks for a cup of coffee?"

Nicky's predictions are so consistently the opposite of the truth that an actor I know often asks him about her movies as a way to gauge their box office appeal. "*Silence of the What?*" I can still hear him ask incredulously.

Ten or so years ago, Best Cellars, a small store on Manhattan's Upper East Side, revolutionized wine sales by grouping wines according to taste ("Fresh," "Juicy," "Big," "Sweet," etc.) rather than by country or grape varietal. Cofounder Joshua Wesson realized that for everyday wine, people were more concerned with what a wine tastes like rather than from which incomprehensible appellation it hails. A radical approach, the strategy was so successful that Best Cellars was bought by the A&P supermarket chain in 2007. The only downside of this super user-friendliness is that it tends to limit the customer it initially seduces. At a certain point, some shoppers—the majority of our customers, we thought— would want to go deeper than "Sweet." If we were going to try to make a unique and better wineshop, we would have to take a more sophisticated tack.

Our first stab was a shop as a wine library. We lined the room's perimeter with floor-to-ceiling bookcases and rolling ladders. We laid out the floor in rows of waist-high bookshelves. We envisioned the doors with copper mesh panels and the woodwork painted glossy gray-green. "Like that store in which Catherine Deneuve worked in the *Umbrellas of Cherbourg*," Becky had remarked. It was all very efficient, very pretty, and, aside from the fancy paint, much like any other liquor store you have ever visited. Walking in, you would have been confronted by thousands of bottles vying for your attention—exactly the intimidating overload we wanted to avoid.

In our next iteration, Becky and I took the opposite approach. Instead of wall-to-wall wine, we decided to highlight a few curated bottles and then create contexts for them to help our customers understand and feel confident about their choices.

We envisioned miniature still lifes in which the bottles would be accompanied by pictures of the winemakers, a review or two pinned up on corkboards, and perhaps even bowls of the grapes from which those particular wines were made. We were valiantly trying to make the point that wine is handmade by real people who have a strong connection to their product. Upon further inspection, we discovered that this precious system would allow us to display a total of eleven bottles at a time. Besides, where in hell were we going to get bunches of Verdicchio grapes in the middle of winter?

I didn't want the store to feel like a museum lesson or an elegant warehouse. I wanted it to evoke the part of my life that I remember from my summers at Villa Cannizzaro, our family's seventeenth-century stone house in Camaiore, a small town outside of Lucca in Tuscany.

For more than thirty years, daily life there had been presided over by my father, Giovanni, a painter turned architect turned painter, and Lisetta, my father's companion. Actually, for most of those years, Lisetta was in charge. Both patrician and energetic, Lisetta is a woman of great culture but blunt. She either loved you—or not.

They met in the early 1970s when my father was recovering from a heart attack at the hospital in nearby Pietrasanta. Lisetta had also suffered one some months earlier, and they were immediately drawn to each other. I guess you could say that their love grew out of two broken hearts.

Lisetta is a natural cook with an encyclopedic knowledge of local dishes. Although we had help, she was often in the kitchen skinning a rabbit that someone had been too slow to prepare or speeding up the pasta prep by churning out a few hundred feather-light gnocchi. One of her biggest fans, my dad was always a *buona forchetta*—a "good fork," or enthusiastic eater.

Lisetta always has the inside scoop, whether sweaters knit by Missoni's sample maker or shoes cobbled at Ferragamo's factory or linen shirts with mother-of-pearl buttons sewn by a sweet signora down the road. Lisetta knows where to source the best pottery in Montelupo, the finest glass in Empoli, the prettiest marble in Vallecchia. She can point you to the best nursery to buy a bougainvillea and the best price on terra-cotta roof tiles. She knows the nondescript storefront behind which to find lambskin suede jackets and the similarly hidden attic from which to source Nepalese cashmere spun in Como. When she is food shopping, local merchants always treat her entrance with a combination of deference and enthusiasm. "Oh, signora!" they say, and then disappear into back rooms to fetch her the freshest Pecorino and the tastiest sausages.

To Lisetta, paying $150 for a bottle of Ornellaia, the famed super-Tuscan red wine, would be equal parts stupidity and bad taste.

Instead, we used to buy our wine in bulk from various family friends. One of our favorites was a Rosso di Montalcino from Cortona. During those summers in the 1970s and 1980s, two things were most memorable: the wine tasted good, even to a disinterested kid/teenager/young adult, and the *damigiana*, equivalent to seventy bottles of wine, was a pain in the butt to heft out of our Fiat. The decanting process was also a messy family project. To keep the wine from spoiling, we bottled it ourselves with supplies from the local *agrario* (farm supply store). Usually,

LISETTA'S SPECIAL SALT

Every time Becky and I leave Cannizzaro to return to New York, Lisetta makes sure we pack some of her herb-infused salt. It's a simple rub she uses for grilled meats such as bistecca alla fiorentina (the heavenly steak made from Tuscany's famed Chianina steers) or rosticciana (the Italian version of spare ribs). At home I also use it as an all-purpose infuser of the taste of home, adding it, for example, to osso bucco or broiled lamb chops. Along with just a drop of her red pepper–infused olive oil, it is a staple that has rescued many a bland meal. Incredibly straightforward, this unpretentious seasoning has a powerful ability to uplift a meal, just like Lisetta herself.

I POUND COARSE SALT
(SEA SALT, IF YOU WANT TO GET FANCY)

3 CLOVES GARLIC

2 SPRIGS FRESH ROSEMARY

SMALL HANDFUL OF SAGE LEAVES

Pour the salt into a large bowl. Finely chop the garlic, rosemary, and sage. Add the chopped mixture to the salt and mix thoroughly. Place in a glass jar or another airtight container. The salt mixture can be used immediately but tastes better with time. Before adding it to meat, pat the meat dry to ensure a crispy crust.

my father would spill and imbibe a fair amount of wine trying to prime the siphon, and we would giggle and everyone left the cellar smiling in wine-splotched clothes. Instead of corks, we sealed each bottle with a tablespoon of our olive oil. (Like corks, olive oil keeps the oxygen from entering the bottle.) Oenophiles will gasp, but because of the oil, we always stored the bottles standing up in the cantina. When we were ready to drink, we used another specialized siphon, a glass bottle with two protruding glass straws, to suck off the oil while leaving the wine undisturbed.

Later, as I learned more about Rosso di Montalcino's more famous brother, Brunello, I used to wonder why my parents were so cheap. Only years later did I realize that the less venerated but also less astringent Rosso was a much tastier everyday wine in addition to being a much better value. Make no mistake: properly aged Brunello, one that has had time for its mouth-puckering tannins to soften into a deep and voluptuous wine, is still one of my favorite treats. But it's the kind of thing I would drink during a romantic tête-à-tête, not with pesto on a weekday night.

Those whom Lisetta loved were equally enrapt with her. In years past, people would start to show up around six o'clock for *aperitivi.* There were writers and poets, painters and sculptors, art critics and museum directors, the foundry owner, the handsome veterinarian (Lisetta loves animals), and always, it seemed, a few kids and someone's elderly *zia* (aunt). On the weekends, dinner was usually for fifteen but could just as easily be for thirty.

At those three-hour meals, wine was hotly debated, but no more than, say, the quality of olive oil or the tastiness of someone's *ragù.* It was part of the same thing, which in turn was just a delicious excuse to bring people together.

Of course, there were some standouts, such as the time my father and Minuccio Cappelli, a Chianti vineyard owner and one of his best pals, shut themselves in the kitchen all day with a few bottles of Cappelli Riserva. What I remember more than the extraordinary food (Marchese Cappelli was called the James Beard of Tuscany) and the passable wine (just because you've had vineyards for three hundred years doesn't make them great) was their muffled chuckles behind the kitchen door and, later, our smiles as we feasted on the fruits of their labor (a titanic cacciucco).

I was not always so gung ho about Italy. When I was a boy, my dad used to send me up the hill to get fresh milk from the farmer. "Why don't we just buy milk in a store like we do in the States?" I'd complain. Nonetheless, every day, I dutifully hiked to the *fattoria* (farm), empty Cynar (an artichoke-based aperitif popular with the older set) bottle in hand. Arriving at the stinky barn (the dairy cows were kept inside in the belief that idle animals made sweeter milk), I'd hold my breath and watch the farmer squeeze the udders and squirt the steaming liquid into the bottle. As soon as he was done, I'd hightail it out of there, sticky bottle in hand, determined never to return. Corn flakes, I should point out, do not taste good with warm milk.

Of course, now I look back on the early morning milk treks with enough fondness to reminisce about them and with the realization that my dad had been on to something that Italians have known all along: the beauty of everyday life lies in rituals like these.

I also fondly remember simple lunches under our pergola, like the ones we continue to have when we visit: fried zucchini

MINUCCIO'S CACCIUCCO
SERVES 6

This Italian version of bouillabaisse is a surprisingly easy feast in one dish. To Minuccio, "assorted fish" meant whatever was caught fresh that day. Much of it was very inexpensive. In his case, the array was likely to include: anguille (eel), calamari (squid), seppie (cuttlefish), cicale (razor clams), arselle (tiny local clams), gamberetti (shrimp), gallinella (sea robin, a crazy-looking fish whose large fins look like wings), palombo (an equally ugly relative of monkfish), nasello (hake), and perhaps something more delicate, such as San Pietro (Saint Peter's fish, or red snapper as a good substitute).

5 POUNDS ASSORTED FISH

SALT AND PEPPER

I LARGE ONION

I OR 2 CELERY STALKS

I CARROT

A HANDFUL OF PARSLEY

I ½ CLOVES GARLIC

3 TO 5 HOT PEPPERS, FINELY CHOPPED

I CUP OLIVE OIL

I BAY LEAF

6 OUNCES RED WINE

I POUND TOMATOES (2 OR 3), ROUGHLY CHOPPED

30 OR SO SLICES OF BREAD, SUCH AS A BAGUETTE, CUT INTO ROUNDS AND TOASTED

I CLOVE GARLIC, SMASHED

Clean the fish (or have it cleaned), cutting off the heads of .the larger ones (reserve the heads!) but keeping the smaller ones intact. If your assortment includes octopus, squid, and/ or cuttlefish, cut them into bite-sized pieces. Season all the seafood with salt and pepper. Finely chop the onion, celery, carrot, and parsley. Set aside. In a small bowl, smash 1½ cloves of garlic and the hot peppers with the back of a spoon, and set aside.

Heat a frying pan to medium-high, then add ½ cup of oil. Sauté the finely chopped onion, celery, carrot, and parsley until the onions are translucent, about 10 minutes. Add the garlic and hot pepper mixture and one whole bay leaf. Sauté for another minute. Toss in the fish heads and cook until the mixture is lightly browned, about 5 minutes (Italians call this stage *imbiondito,* or blond). Pour in the wine, and cook slowly until the alcohol has evaporated. Then add the tomatoes, cover, and simmer for 30 minutes. Remove the garlic and bay leaf. Strain through a mesh sieve, and set the sauce aside.

Put the remaining ½ cup of oil in a large casserole and, if your selection includes octopus, squid, and/or cuttlefish, add them to the pot. Pour in the reserved sauce, add 2 cups of water, cover, and simmer for 15 minutes.

While the fish is simmering, preheat the oven to 350°F. Rub the bread slices with the smashed garlic clove. Arrange the rounds on a baking sheet and toast them until brown, 1 to 2 minutes. Flip over the slices and cook for another min-

(recipe continues)

ute. Turn off the oven, leaving the rounds inside the oven to keep warm.

Add the sturdier fish (e.g., monkfish, eel) to the casserole dish, and after 5 minutes add the more delicate fish (such as red snapper). Simmer for an additional 10 minutes. Taste and season with salt and pepper, if necessary. Serve the cacciucco in bowls over the toasted garlic bread rounds.

Enjoy with a bottle of Candia dei Colli Apuani. Though it was not from his vineyards, Minuccio and my father liked this local white wine grown in the hills between Tuscany and Liguria to the north. Blended from Vermentino, Trebbiano, and Albarola, Candia is a refreshing, unpretentious white that complements the delicate seafood.

---

blossoms, fried cod, fresh caciotta from the remote Garfagnana area of northeastern Tuscany, a few leaves of salad from our garden drizzled with a few drops of our own olive oil, a bowlful of tiny and incredibly fragrant wild strawberries, and a glass of light Camaiorese red. I wanted the wineshop to embody this easy relationship between wine and food and sociability. The only trick was finding a way to underscore that connection without illegally serving food and wine in a retail store!

Becky and I decided to forgo extra storage in favor of creating an *enoteca*, or tasting room, in the rear of the wineshop. With thirteen-foot ceilings and heavy beams, the space already had good bones. From a local quarry that used to supply bluestone for the sidewalks of New York, we installed a bluestone floor and added pairs of steel French doors that open onto a small garden on which my mother-in-law lavishes attention.

When I was young, I had always dreamed, as many New Yorkers do, of opening up the closet door and finding an extra bedroom that I had never known existed. Off a boarded-up street and tucked behind the store, the enoteca became that secret hideaway.

Our fondness for Italy is how I rationalized the choice to put a car, my 1967 Ferrari 330 GT, in the middle of the store. Yes, plunking a sixteen-foot-long vehicle in the middle of our selling floor made no real economic sense. But with its wire wheels and wooden steering wheel, the 1960's Ferrari symbolized a carefree, dolce vita dream—exactly how the store should feel and, in my mind's eye, what I wanted my life to become. Home above, store below. Working with wine at my fingertips and a dog at my feet.

As a child, not everything I learned about wine was from Italy. My mother, a New Yorker by way of Baltimore, loved good wine but hated pretension. At our home on Manhattan's Upper West Side, Mom preferred Gigondas, the hearty Rhône red, to its more famous neighbor Châteauneuf-du-Pape; white Burgundy Meursault to more headline-grabbing Montrachet; Beaumes de Venises to the more prestigious Sauternes. She liked to appreciate the overshadowed, and this may explain why I feel comfortable offering under-the-radar wines in the store.

As my father spent more time in Italy with Lisetta, Mom encouraged experimentation. In the 1970s, she allowed her ten-year-old to collect *digestivi* in miniature bottles and to "taste test" thimblefuls of those bitter herbal concoctions side by side.

I think she'd smile if she knew that thirty years later I would still be playing a version of that game.

My mom was also the only non-wine professional I have ever met who could recite the Bordeaux Classification of 1855, the five-tiered wine-ranking system.

Although she had advanced Alzheimer's disease by the time we conceived of the store; Mom's informed, but relaxed, approach to wine pervades the place.

Becky's boss, Martha Stewart, reminds me a lot more of Lisetta than of my mom. Both Martha and Lisetta meld bluntness and brisk efficiency with a sense of style and a captivating persona. Yet both women melt around animals. Coincidentally, Martha used to rent a house in Camaiore, our tiny Italian town.

I don't want you to get the wrong idea: despite her being my wife's employer of more than ten years, Martha and I are not exactly bosom buddies. But her point of view permeated our store vision almost as much as Lisetta's. Martha edits. She hones. She is relentless. With over twenty-four thousand domestic and international wines available in this country, we knew we had a lot to sift through. And we would have to be as demanding as Becky's boss.

The other Martha message, by way of Mies van der Rohe, the modernist architect, is that details matter. It's not enough to have a hazy sketch of an idea. You must fill it in with the same conviction as the big picture. Martha is why we use the perfect saddle-stitched chocolate brown grosgrain ribbon to wrap bottles; why we have a cork business card that's also a magnet; why our gift cards are engraved with calligraphic fish.

One of the most attractive qualities about Martha is her insatiable curiosity. She loves an expert and will ask question after question, as Ryan Ibsen, our wine director can attest. She's a great interrogator and can sift quickly, probe, find the secret. For Martha, we reminded ourselves, every day is an opportunity to learn more.

We had a lot to learn about wine and also, as it turns out, about parenting: in October 2004, we discovered that the co-founder of our soon-to-be shop (Becky) was pregnant with a boy. At least our dream now had a name, Pasanella & Son.

As her belly grew, so did our anxiety. Among the biggest open questions: Who were we going to get to run this money-sucking enterprise? Then, as if scripted, came a fateful encounter on a last-minute run to Whole Foods.

I was preparing for Becky's thirtieth birthday and ran out to pick up a loaf of bread and a few odds and ends. I left Whole Foods with more than $200 worth of cheese thanks to the energetic sales clerk behind the counter.

"You know that Tomme would go perfectly with a bottle of slightly chilled Chinon," she suggested. "I have a fresh wheel in the back."

"Okay," I murmured.

She continued: "And that Burgundy you mentioned would be amazing with a Pavé d'Auge!"

"How do you know all of this?" I asked as she bent down behind the counter and I noticed a pair of tattooed wings on her back.

"Oh, I worked at Acker and Sotheby's," she replied, lifting up the wheel.

The rest is a blur of farmstead Cheddars and artisan robiola. I left feeling charmed—and a little bit fleeced.

The day after Becky's party (where the pairings were a huge

hit), I returned to the cheese counter and asked the cheese whiz, Janet Hoover, if she would be interested in helping me set up a wineshop. "Just a part-time gig, but—" At which point she practically tore off her apron and leapt over the counter.

I set up a small office on the second floor, in the room where the fish guys used to have the knife-studded and cash-strewn table. With demolition below and the fish market in full swing outside, the environment was chaotic, but Janet was driven. We had never heard someone rattle on more quickly about point-of-sale systems, delivery trucks, and must-have wines. Janet's to-do list was six pages long and in a constant state of revision, studded with yellow highlights and Post-it note addenda. We were alternately awed and exhausted by her fervor.

One of Janet's first triumphs was to introduce us to her beau, Jude Wessex, who was head of auctions for a large wineshop and auction house. Jude was invaluable. He shared spreadsheets that revealed the inner workings of a great retail store. Jude and Janet told us where the money was made (cheap Pinot Grigio), what percentage of our budget should be for Chianti (not much), and how long it would take us to turn over 100 cases of vodka (about a year and a half).

Jude invited me to my first wine auction, which was held at New York's Cru restaurant. As Janet and I made our way past the eatery's Fifth Avenue entrance, we were ushered in as if we were Beyoncé and Jay-Z. Besides Janet and a vaguely familiar, bone-thin Russian model, the room was filled with puffed men with I-know-better-than-you swagger. It was like being at a high rollers' table in Las Vegas. The food was extravagant—foie gras, caviar-stuffed beggar's purses—and ignored. The wines were serious and also, apparently, took a backseat to the action, which consisted of idly thumbing through the glossy catalogue as you glanced at who was at the other tables. Janet had prepped beforehand (perhaps with help from Jude) and had her wish list and ceiling prices ready to go. We bought $5,000 worth (a pittance for the real players) but came home with some rare and desirable wine for the store: The Maiden from Harlan, among the most coveted California Cabernets; Two Hands Lily's Garden, an Australian wine with a cult following; Vieux Château Certan, a perennial Bordeaux heavy hitter; and Feudi San Gregorio Serpico 2001, a "staggeringly rich" (according to famed critic Robert Parker), almost impossible to source, 98-point-rated southern Italian red.

Gamesmanship aside, it also became clear that provenance was a critical factor in determining value. Many of the lots belonged to the "cellar of an esteemed collector," which meant that they could have just as likely been sitting on someone's kitchen counter for years before they were consigned. Real insiders knew who was an "esteemed collector" and who had been given a Christmas bonus he never drank.

Through Jude, we also found a Manhattan liquor attorney, Stew Burg, whom we hired to shepherd our license application. Arriving at Burg's office, I introduced myself to the receptionist through a Plexiglas barrier with a hole in it. A few minutes later, a slightly shambling figure emerged. Burg is retained because of his connections to the New York State Liquor Authority board members. Jude told us that you hire Stew because he has those commissioners in his pocket.

So I did what Stew told me: I got myself fingerprinted and photographed, paid $1,000 to a bond company (still not exactly

sure why), attached a lease, appended a store diagram, and submitted a notarized statement from me (landlord) vouching for
me (tenant) along with the fifty-two-page liquor license application (a form designed to ferret out mobsters with questions such
as "Have all investors been disclosed in this application? Yes or
No") to the New York State Liquor Authority. The SLA website
explained that we should expect to wait about three months.

Meanwhile, we had our hands full. On June 17, 2005, Becky
gave birth to our Luca, the "Son" in Pasanella & Son. And for
most of the summer we were more preoccupied with milk (and
diapers) than with wine. Luca's thirst also meant that my most
trusted taster was out of commission for three months.

In August, almost three months to the day we applied for the
liquor license, I got a call from Stew announcing that we would
be required to appear at a perfunctory hearing the following
week. At the hearing, our seasoned liquor attorney explained, he
would get up and describe why it would "serve the public interest" to open our store. Up we trekked to 126th Street and Lenox
Avenue, the headquarters of an agency responsible for $206 mil-
lion in annual tax revenue.

The hearing room featured a long table with tented legs behind which sat the board. Before us was an earnest couple looking for a license for their organic restaurant and a grocer seeking
a beer license in Queens. They all were nervous, and both were
quickly approved. When our turn came, Stew did his three-
minute spiel about this young couple looking to open a wineshop
in their own building in Manhattan's Seaport Historic District.
As Stew made his way back down the aisle, one of the commissioners offhandedly asked, in the manner of a minister at a wedding, "Any objections?"

Hands shot up. A trio of downtown liquor store owners with handwritten scripts rushed to the podium to protest that we would put them out of business. Their comments were peppered with "9/11" and "Ground Zero." Our shop, they argued, would be the "final nail in the coffin." One speaker in particular, the son of a package store owner, was so moving that he even had me choked up. I almost forgot that his father's place, a block from the former World Trade Center, was almost a mile away in lower Manhattan, where the population density hovers around 750,000 people per square mile.

There were murmurs among the commissioners and then the announcement: "License deferred."

"Deferred?!" I screamed in my head.

Stew nodded and said nothing.

Where, I wondered, was my tireless advocate, my Atticus Finch? Where, I wanted to know, was my friggin' Mr. Inside!?

We limped out of the meeting, and I was convinced that what Stew called a "hiccup" was going to require some real work on my part.

It was remarkable that none of the commissioners were from New York City. To these upstate guys, I realized, almost a mile seemed pretty close.

I asked Janet to take our video camera and walk at a normal pace from our building to the two nearest liquor stores. She left our cobbled Seaport Historic District, crossed Water Street, and went up the hill and through the canyons of office buildings. Twenty minutes later, she reached the second store. I sent DVDs to each commissioner. Again I waited.

Weeks passed. The delay was probably not due to bureaucratic ineptitude. What we did not know was that the SLA had been drafted by the attorney general to assist in a major investigation of the local wine and spirits business. In November 2005, Eliot Spitzer, the ardent New York State attorney general, launched an inquiry into unfair wholesale pricing.

Spitzer alleged that the major distributors offered discounts and free merchandise to preferred stores as well as to favored bars, restaurants, and nightclubs. The minor payola, the attorney general contended, included gifts such as iPods and vacation trips. The big numbers were funneled in more creative ways. Large retailers, I later learned, had set up shell marketing companies to receive payments for ads in their mail-order catalogs. If you saw a full-page spread for a name brand in a store circular, chances were that it was a paid advertisement. Spitzer also alleged that some wholesalers bought gift cards from those customers ($400,000 worth in one case).

Although the investigation was good news for small retailers like me, secretly, I was less than horrified by what it had revealed. Practices Spitzer described as dastardly ("Kickbacks!" "Payola!") sounded pretty mundane when I thought of them as discounts and perks to preferred customers. Not surprisingly, the big guy was getting the best price. As the *New York Sun* argued in a November 14, 2005, editorial, these deals may be unsavory, might even be illegal, but certainly were not as criminal as, say, Medicaid fraud.

That fall, while Spitzer was rounding up bad guys and we were waiting anxiously for the license, we started drinking with purpose. We may not yet have had the official go-ahead, but we had a store to fill and had to figure out what to sell.

It soon became clear that Janet, the daughter of a religious studies professor and a pious mother, bowed to one God: French Burgundy. One of the first times we tasted with her was on the second floor amid the stacks of computer boxes, the unopened cash register tapes, and the scattered wine cases. On top of her paper-strewn desk, she uncorked a 1999 Armand Rousseau Gevrey-Chambertin, an excellent year for a signature wine of an esteemed winemaker. And if what followed was not exactly seeing the eye of God, it was an epiphany.

Janet poured and swirled.

And lingered.

She closed her eyes.

She coddled the glass.

She inhaled and sighed a half dozen times.

Becky and I looked at each other dumbfounded. "*This* is who you hired?" I could hear my wife silently asking.

But the smell—no, the aroma—was captivating. Woodsy, mushroomy, and wet, it reminded me of walking through the chestnut forests behind our house in Italy. More oohs and aahs followed after her first sips. We dived in. I was really concentrating. It was complicated. The taste was feral but refined. For the first time, I was listening to a wine. And all of a sudden it occurred to me: this is sexy. Becky was smiling too.

For someone used to washing down *tordelli* (a Tuscan meat-filled ravioli) with a back-slapping Chianti, the first real tasting was a lot like discovering another virtual room. I had been drinking wine all my life but had never really tasted it until this point.

There's an industry saying that it takes eight years for a wine drinker to mature from predominantly cheap and simple Australian Shiraz to almost exclusively expensive and nuanced French

Burgundy. In the five years that have passed, I have discovered many wines that I like as much as, but none more than, a fine Burgundy.

Over time, our tastings became more frequent, and occasionally as compelling, but one thing was soon clear: Becky has a much better nose than I do. She could down ten Pinot Grigios and pick the best almost without thinking. Even though I had grown up in a wine culture, had read all those wine books (Hugh Johnson's encyclopedic *Atlas of Wine,* the equally exhaustive *The Oxford Companion to Wine,* Clive Coates's *Wines of Burgundy,* and all the Robert Parker books among them), and wanted to be good, I still lagged behind her. I could pick the coolest or the most revered wine, but I could not tell you the best. My palate was color-blind: I could make out the outlines, but I was missing the substance.

It didn't help that Janet was soon taking me to dinners among the wine-obsessed, where she inevitably would show off. One of her favorite parlor tricks was to blind taste a bottle in front of a group of wine collectors and then identify not only the region and grape but also the winemaker and the year.

At a dinner in the Chelsea loft of a pianist and his companion, we were treated to a harpsichord recital while bottle after bottle was swaddled in cloths and laid out in a line on the dining table. By the time the recital had finished, I stumbled to my chair, having reached my two-drink limit (yes, this liquor store owner is a cheap date). Janet, who had downed the same two glasses of Chablis, was raring to go. The first bottle was full-bodied, red, ripe, and deep. I could taste the fruit. Janet took a few swirls and took a stab: "Rhône, possibly Crozes-Hermitage. . . ."

Then a few more sips. "Chave, 2001!" she declared, flashing

purple-stained teeth as surely as if she were saying her own name.

That is exactly what the pianist revealed when he took the cloth off the label.

Whoa.

With a few years' hindsight, Janet's apparent miracle now seems more Sherlock Holmes than Amazing Kreskin. With practice, grape varietals offer telltale signs: Cabernet Franc, for example, tends to be herby, Zinfandel is peppery, and Syrah, the predominant grape in a southern Rhône wine, often tastes deep and full-bodied with hints of what critics like to term "black fruit" (plums, currants). Janet also may have been tipped off by the bottle's shape, with its long, sloping shoulders. Then again, Australian Shiraz (another name for the same grape) can come in a similarly shaped bottle, although the Shiraz tends to be made in a more extroverted style. Syrah is garrulous French; Shiraz is loud Aussie. Janet probably could have excluded the Australian, as well as its so-called "New World" (any place other than Europe) brethren, because there was just a hint of the oakiness that often characterizes these wines. Knowing that the hosts were avid collectors and assuming that the wine was delicious, it was not a far leap to assume that they would have bought from one of the most renowned of that region's producers, Jean-Louis Chave. Janet could also tell—as a novice wine taster also would be able to recognize—that the wine was old enough to have lost its mouth-puckering tannins but not so old to have turned brownish. Finally, 2001 was also a terrific year. And so, voilà.

Janet had a great palate, and I enjoyed sharing in the blind-tasting miracles, but more and more I was realizing that they were more the result of common sense and practice than the hand of God.

By late fall 2005, a little divine intervention would have been appreciated as we continued to languish in liquor license purgatory. Janet was starting to get antsy. With her to-do list shrinking, our dynamo started arriving a little later each day. In the afternoons, she disappeared to meet distributors, ostensibly to taste more wines. Inevitably when she returned after several hours, flashing those purple teeth, I would be irritated. "Kid," I thought to myself, "you're getting tipsy on my dime." Then again, I reasoned, she needed to sample as much as she could to be the best buyer for me, so I held my tongue.

In the worst-case scenario, I was okay with our having spent months tasting (not exactly an unpleasant way to pass one's time), but I had promised myself that I would not start construction until I knew we had the license. Yet we desperately wanted to open by the holidays as Jude had let us know that 60 percent of a shop's annual sales come between Thanksgiving and New Year's Eve. Pressure was mounting. I was starting to feel like a cane on a vine that was yet to sprout. I realized that if we waited any longer, we would miss the lucrative holiday season. So we leaped again.

I quickly submitted plans to the buildings department. While I waited for the permits, I hired someone to smooth out the pitched floor—great for washing away fish guts but not so nice for tile. The more he chiseled, the more we discovered just how badly the concrete tilted. It soon became clear that we would have to jackhammer the whole floor to get it smooth.

With my fifteen years of practice in design, you would have thought that I could be a better manager of the construction process. That was the point at which I should have said, "Let's just wait until we get the approval."

Instead, we continued jackhammering until one of our tenants dialed New York City's 311 complaint hotline to report a building on the verge of collapse. The inspector made a beeline for our place and told me what I already knew: I was no longer making a repair but putting in a new floor that would require a demolition permit. I had to stop immediately and pay an I-do-not-want-to-remember-how-much fine.

When the stop work order was lifted, I proceeded to make matters worse. Concerned that my two-man crew would not be able to finish the store by December, I phoned one of the carpenters with whom I had worked at the Maritime. The "sailor," as he was called, had made the curtains for the Manhattan Japanese restaurant Matsuri by tying nautical knots. I needed a guy with that kind of ingenuity. And the sailor was cool. He had traveled the world by boat, opened a restaurant during one of his layovers in Paraguay, and kept a yawl in City Island. He was an accomplished carpenter and an inveterate spinner of yarns, no doubt honed on those long ocean voyages. I was smitten.

Within days after giving the sailor a deposit, it became clear that in addition to being a world-class seaman, he was a big mistake for this job. The mariner loved to sail but, apparently, not much else. A boat bum, he took advantage of every freebie, drinking bottle after bottle of the Poland Spring we had stockpiled upstairs. The seafarer would disappear at lunchtime and return with bloodshot eyes. He would make a big show of walking around with some piece of molding and then take a couple of hours to cut it in half. Despite his facility with things nautical, the sailor did not really know the first thing about creating a watertight storefront. In fact, he forgot to install the weatherproofing. The seaman's cohort, a Vespa-riding hipster, it soon became apparent, was similarly unmotivated and semicompetent. My back was against the wall.

Just as the store was starting to come together, the city announced that the fish market would be leaving by the end of the year. "It's done," Vinnie notified me one day as I stood outside the building, waiting once again for the sailor to show up. "We're finally moving." "When?" I asked. "Two weeks. That's it." Vinnie seemed in no mood to talk.

I felt caught. Although I was relieved to be rid of that 4 a.m. racket and thrilled not to have to hop over puddles of snapper guts, I was sad about losing the fraternity of fish guys who had adopted me and was depressed at the prospect of an eviscerated neighborhood. In its waning days, the market workers were listless, too. The ice man, the forklift operators, and Pushcart Annie, who for more than fifty years sold black market cigarettes from her shopping cart, seemed to be dragging their rubber boots more slowly over the fish scales, crushed ice, and discarded packing straps that littered the streets.

For 183 years, the market had managed to remain in place even though the fish no longer came there by boat. It had outlasted fifty-seven mayors. It had survived 9/11 and Giuliani and fifteen years of city announcements of its pending move. Now its time had come. At sunrise, on their last morning, I saw Vinnie's hulking lieutenant, his scruffy beard hidden under a weather-beaten balaclava, staring out toward the river with a tear streaming down his cheek, just like the stalwart Native American in the 1970's littering commercial.

A week later, a fat envelope—the kind you want to get when you've been accepted to college—arrived containing the liquor license. It was going to be a while before I came through on my promises to visit the fish guys in the Bronx. With two weeks left until the year's end, we decided to open up a small part of the store while the rest of the space was under construction. A few days before Christmas, with many bottles covered in dust and in the middle of a transit strike, we cracked open the door. We were in business at last.

chapter 3

HARVEST

THE ABUNDANCE OF HARVEST festivals leads one to believe that the reaping season is a time of irrepressible joy. After months of pampering and prodding, the grapes are finally safe. But before you can dance under the full moon, you have to worry, especially if you are in the wine business.

For grape growers, the harvest is about timing. It's not enough to select plump fruit with good color as you would in a supermarket. Winemakers crave perfect sugar and tannin levels. Sugar determines the alcohol content of the finished wine. Tannins, those mouth-puckering compounds, are the key to a wine's structure and ageability. Jump the gun and the overeager producer may end up with tart fruit and, subsequently, weak, low-alcohol wine. The brew is likely to be bitter too. Wait too long—the difference can be a day in the fast-ripening summer heat—and the inattentive grower may end up with the opposite: overripe grapes bursting with sugar that make overly alcoholic, or "hot," wines. Or worse, one late rainstorm followed by a steamy spell can jump-start mold and ruin the whole crop.

With stakes this high, leave it to the amateurs to howl at

the moon. Seasoned winemakers recognize that the harvest is just the beginning of the journey.

"*J*ANET QUIT," BECKY whispered to me as I lined up the last bottle on a display. Three hundred guests (including friends, former clients, Martha Stewart, and Florence Fabricant of the *New York Times*) were arriving in ten minutes, and we had no wine director for the grand opening of Pasanella & Son. Becky knew I would freak, and so she calmly delivered the news in her best soothing voice.

"She what?! You've got to be f'ing kidding!" I screamed as I backed into the display.

In the movies, accidents always seem to happen in slow motion. In our case, what followed was an instant smack of glass against tile and a simultaneous explosion of Nero d'Avola. The display collapsed, and the table laden with rosemary focaccia was sodden; sharp slivers had fallen onto the hand-sliced salumi, puddles were forming around the front counter, and my opening-night shirt—the silky Italian one I had worn for our wedding—was spattered with the inky Sicilian red.

It was February 2006, many notable New Yorkers were arriving at our doorstep for the unveiling of our new venture, and our whiz kid wine director was not to be found. But given the bleary-eyed late morning entrances and extended afternoon MIAs, it shouldn't have been a surprise. The eight months it took to get the store up and running had tried Janet's patience. As a bike messenger, she had been able to bomb down the street to get the job done. At Whole Foods, she just needed to carve another hunk of Parmigiano to finish the sale. In contrast, our new

venture demanded planning and patience. With her impulsive-
ness stymied, our speed-talking wine buyer was bouncing off the
walls. We should have known.

With the public relations firm's clipboard girls and their plug-
in headsets arrayed in front of the store, ready to check in the expected throngs, this was no time to philosophize. What I needed
was a mop.

We all pitched in, and within minutes the store looked pristine once again. The room was soon full of cheerful bonhomie
and the hearty laughs that come from fine wine, tasty food, and
good company.

In addition to the tables laden with six-foot-long focaccie,
we set up a few games. In the enoteca, we laid out "Spin the
Salami." Lucky winners got to kiss Becky, and losers got to peck
me. Toward the front of the shop, we set up a mirrored chess-
board with wineglass playing pieces (white versus red) that I had
made. There were piles of creamy Gorgonzola, translucent slices
of salumi, and mounds of grapes.

We had even arranged with Pietro Romanengo, a Genovese
candy maker that first opened its doors in 1780, to fly in an impeccably presented assortment of candied quinces, sugar-coated
orange peels, and chartreuse cordial drops.

All the expected notables showed, including some from the
wine world. There was the chortling older gentleman gorging on
amuse-bouches and washing everything down with Côte du Nu-
its. There were a few bearded hipsters, sniffing and spitting and
dissecting each selection with their wine-stained fingers. There
were neighbors, friends, acquaintances, and semistrangers. Everyone was grinning. At the end of the night, Becky, rolling up
the chocolate-brown waxed paper tablecloths, and I, munching

on remnants of zucchini pizza, glanced across the banged-up flower arrangements and mountains of half-empty glasses and gave each other high fives with our eyes. This crazy, happy night was exactly what we had dreamed of—only better.

We felt so good that we actually accepted Janet's plea to "un-quit" the next day. In subsequent weeks, there were newspaper mentions and blog posts. Six months after we opened, *New York* magazine named us "Best Neighborhood Wine Shop." The most otherworldly accolade that followed was an eight-page feature in *Food & Wine* titled "An American Lives the Tuscan Dream," which opened with a cheerful family portrait: an angelic six-month-old Luca flanked by his radiant mother and me, paunchy but beaming. The article described the charmed life of our young family. It made no mention of the mortgage or the fish smell.

While the press flowed, we had to get back to work and I had to learn the wine business. I was ready to hang a silver cup around my neck and hop a flight to Paris. I fantasized about spending my days moseying from vineyard to vineyard, finding wines for the store. Friends thought I'd be devoting my time to rooting around moist eighteenth-century caves looking for hidden stashes of 1961 Pomerol, coveted Bordeaux from one of the legendary vintages of the twentieth century. Or I would be lurching from one wine-soaked, three-hour vineyard lunch to another, tasting, toasting, and, occasionally, napping.

As if.

The truth is that winery visits are more ceremonial than necessary. Yes, producers tend to welcome me warmly, particularly if we've been selling a lot of their wine. But I don't make big deals among ancient oak barrels, nor do I discover caches of legendary vintages in cobwebbed cellars. Instead, I buy from sales reps who show up at my shop with flight attendant luggage filled with bottles of sample wines.

In New York, wine and liquor are sold through a three-tier system: winemaker sells to distributor (1) who sells to me (2) and then on to you (3). If the wine is foreign, it must come through an importer, which adds yet another link in the chain. With their Prohibition-era roots, the Alcoholic Beverage Control (ABC) laws were intended to ensure the state its share of taxes by using a wholesaler to guarantee their collection. Officially (we'll get to that part later), wine can only be sold through wholesalers by these traveling salespeople.

In our store, we see reps on Wednesday afternoons and the staff tastes together. When the eager salespeople pile up in the front of the store trailed by their bottle-filled bags, the shop starts to look like the waiting room of a regional airport.

The first sales rep I remember meeting was Armando Arroyo, a former sommelier at the New York restaurant Daniel and star salesman for Michael Skurnik, a fine wine distributor, whose brands include the noted Barbaresco producer Moccagatta and the cult California winemaker Peter Michael. As he rested his hand on my shoulder, Armando talked with ease about the legendary names in his portfolio. He lined up a dozen bottles to "taste through," as they say in the trade. There was a Selbach-Oster Riesling (a quintessential German wine from one of the finest producers in the Mosel Valley) and a Vincent Dampt Chablis (an equally classic French Burgundy from the latest generation of a storied family). Despite the offhand presentation, both wines were carefully culled middle-range offerings from well-regarded vintners. All the while, Armando spoke with the ease of someone who had known me for years. I later discovered that reps typically start with their simplest and lightest wines and finish with something phenomenal and way beyond the shop owner's price range. In this case, it was a La Spinetta Barbaresco 1997, a blockbuster Italian red from a stellar year priced at approximately $200. "And why don't you keep this to drink tonight?" he suggested.

The next day, I was nervous to meet our rep from Southern Wine & Spirits, the nation's largest distributor, which had just barreled into the New York City market. Southern had consistently expanded and then dominated each new market. It grew from a one-man shop in 1968 to a national powerhouse representing over five thousand brands in thirty-eight states. Even before it came to New York in 2004, Southern was selling $5.5 billion of wine and liquor per year.

This time they had expanded not just to seize an opportunity but, apparently, to settle a score. A few years earlier, Charmer Sunbelt, the biggest New York–based distributor, had allegedly violated a gentleman's agreement by opening a distributorship in Florida, Southern's home turf. According to a former sales manager for one of Southern's fine wine divisions, the move was due to Charles Merinoff, the overreaching son of Charmer CEO Herman Merinoff, who could not resist the temptation to expand their empire. "That kid could fuck up a wet dream," the pinkie-ringed former manager told me. Southern, also run by a father-and-son team, Harvey and Wayne Chaplin, purportedly saw betrayal.

For the next two years, the manager averred, Southern plotted revenge. They studied the New York market. They identified the best salespeople, the proven brands, and the key accounts. Then, in 2004, they pounced. According to a lawsuit filed by Charmer in 2005, Southern quickly made off with twenty-five key employees, supposedly even going so far as to offer a $5 million signing bonus to one particularly valuable recruit. In quick succession, Southern also acquired the exclusive regional distribution rights to such cash-cow brands as Absolut vodka and Plymouth gin. They followed by picking up a prestigious wine importer, Lauber. In describing their New York arrival, *Wine Business Monthly* said Southern "steamrolled" into the market with "military precision." The New York wine and spirits business had not seen such upheaval since Prohibition.

Instead of Darth Vader, in walked Matt Moriarty, the soft-spoken Southern salesman with tousled hair. Wearing a too-large suit, Matt, it turned out, was a French wine fan who made custom guitars in his spare time. From his wheelie bag, he wowed us with selections from two superstar Italian producers: Silvio Jermann and Feudi di San Gregorio. Hardly what you would expect from the Evil Empire.

Scion of a Friulian vineyard founded in 1881, Jermann revolutionized the wines from that northeastern Italian region best known for its lean white wines. Fond of inventive blends, Jermann resurrected long-forgotten native varietals such as Pignolo (literally, "fussy," which seems apt given its reputation for low and uneven yields) and Malvasia Istriana (a local variety from Istria, a peninsula east of Trieste that Italians still rue having ceded after World War II) to create dense, complex wines. Like a mad scientist, the reclusive Jermann is reputed to be so enamored of the alchemy of winemaking that he is rarely seen outside the vineyard. The names Jermann gives to the family wines have only cemented his idiosyncratic reputation. "Were Dreams" is what he calls one of his most famous whites. The title is a nod to the U2 song—Jermann is a big fan—"Where the Streets Have No Name." Rich, pure, and fanatically well made, Jermann's wines are among the most expensive and sought-after Italian whites.

For those who associate southern Italian reds with cheap and cheerful, Feudi San Gregorio is a similar revelation. Gregorio is famous for coaxing Aglianico, a southern Italian grape varietal that can be bitter and recalcitrant, to produce powerful and mysterious reds that are as impressive as Jermann's bewitching whites. These are also not cheap wines. We happily ordered both wines on offer.

For months, Matt came to our shop weekly, whereas most of the other reps dropped by once a month. I was always charmed by his knowledgeable but self-effacing manner. He was always very prepared, yet with a surprise, and never pushed anything in a jug. Only later did I figure out that Janet had encouraged his frequent visits because she had a crush on him.

In reality, the Charmer reps were scarier. They had some brand-name wines, but Charmer's bread and butter was booze. Their salespeople were interchangeable guys named Vinnie touting specials on blueberry-flavored vodka. Invariably, they showed up unannounced to "move product." "You gotta try this stuff," they said. "Awesome!" "Whoa, talk about a Jell-O shot!" Rather than gifting 2005 bottles of Vieux Telegraphe, the storied French Rhône wine from a legendary year, these guys forked over fistfuls of airline-sized sample bottles "fuh laytah."

The worst thing I ever tasted came from a two-man band of Argentinean entrepreneurs. The duo offered Chilean and Argentinean wines in a market awash in mass-market South American

Malbecs, an often bitter French varietal. Explosively popular in the last five years, Argentinean Malbecs tend to be plush wines with deep colors, intense fruit flavors, and velvety textures. With imports up over 60 percent in 2008, these inexpensive and unsophisticated crowd-pleasers are available through big distributors. To sip most Malbecs is to be charmed by a South American playboy's stories, only to realize that he really has only one lovely anecdote repeated over and over again.

South America has a reputation for blockbuster wines: robust reds and oaky whites. The gregariousness of those wines is due in part to the warm climate, which makes for big, ripe grapes, and in part to what they perceive as American demand for heavy-handed flavors. Rarely would you mistake a Chilean white for a Grüner Veltliner, the light Austrian wine.

Although Victor, the front man, hawked like a guy eager to move merchandise falling off the back of a truck, he also promised something that no one else had: a crisp, refreshing white that he tantalizingly described as a "South American Sancerre."

"Ju are going to luf this," Victor promised as he flashed the bottle. What he then so proudly uncorked was a Torrontés, a white varietal indigenous to Argentina that just happens to be my least favorite grape of all time. To date, I have never tasted a Torrontés that I would want to have on my table or at my shop. I took a fat swish. The world's foulest wine tasted like acetone flavored with grape SweeTart. I never before spit with such authority.

On a slow afternoon, a polite twentysomething woman with what my mom would call a "heaving bosom" strolled in and poured glass after glass directly in front of her revealing blouse. As she talked, I tried to ask smart questions, staring intently at the price list. A few days later, another rep poured an entire lineup in front of a bursting boob backdrop. By the time I met the husky-voiced blonde with the plunging neckline, I was starting to feel self-conscious. "Don't look," I told myself, only to find myself hypnotized by her cleavage magnified through the half-filled glasses. Over the following months, even more of these well-spoken and well-endowed reps showed up. If the typecasting hadn't been so consistent, it would have been hard to believe. What made these sexy sales calls all the more confusing is that the tight-shirted sales staff was spread among some of the best distributors in the business. "Do the world's most prestigious wines," I asked myself, "really sell better framed between a woman's breasts?" Sure seems like they do.

A few months after our initial visit, Armando, the salesman who had given me that $200 bottle of Barbaresco, returned, this time introducing us to a shy Piedmontese winemaker, Fabio Burlotto. The latest generation to take the helm of one of the oldest-school Barolo producers, Fabio filled us in on the two-hundred-year-old family business that had been the favored supplier to the former king of Italy but never managed to make the cover of *Wine Spectator*. Fabio kept his head down, and so I hardly noticed his wall eye. Trying to catch his gaze, all I could see were his Hermès sneakers.

Armando, in contrast, was beaming. He had a trophy vintner whom he had no doubt been dragging from retailer to retailer. These "work-withs," I have discovered, are about as fun for the producers as dental surgery. The winemakers are forced to hawk their wares, numbingly repeating the same polished anecdotes. These chestnuts inevitably include a touching moment with a grandfather walking through the vineyards as a child or a more salacious one with a girlfriend (who later becomes a wife) among the same vines. Then the rep hands over the price sheet and gives the buyer (me) the "So?" look.

Fabio clearly knew the drill and wanted it to be painless and quick. He dutifully laid out a line of bottles featuring old-fashioned black script over white labels. Elegant, understated, humble. Just like the winemaker himself. Our first taste was of a local and lesser-known varietal called Pelaverga.

"Virgin skin," Armando added lasciviously, providing a loose translation.

In spite of Armando's leering, the wine was delicate and mysterious. It rewarded attention by unfolding as you let it linger on your tongue. I am sure we also tasted some of Fabio's blockbuster Barolos that day, but what I remember most clearly is his quiet wine made from a heretofore unheard of varietal.

Other winemakers followed, towed by eager sales reps. None had quite as much impact as Stephane Tissot. "I'm not going to imagine you naked," I repeated to myself as Tissot walked into our store, one of the most ardent adherents of biodynamic winemaking, rumored to pick all his grapes in the buff. But as a relative newbie to the wine world, I was keen on hearing more about the cutting-edge viticultural techniques practiced by this well-known French producer, who runs the family domaine in the foothills of the Alps with his wife, Bénédicte. And here he was standing in the back of my new wineshop with a grinning rep by his side.

In the last few years, the market for biodynamic wines has skyrocketed. In Pasanella & Son's first year, we had had only one inquiry about biodynamic wines. Now we field at least one question a day. When new customers come to the store, I now see them scanning the labels and letting out satisfied "hmmms" when they see the "bio" symbol. Our current bestselling white, an Austrian Grüner Veltliner, is biodynamic.

The popularity of these seemingly über-green wines is not limited to independent shops in New York. National chains have reported similar spikes. The *Minneapolis Star-Tribune* calls the sales growth of these wines "explosive." The ever-prescient Berrys' recently launched a wine blog, *Wine Matters,* devoted entirely to biodynamic wines.

Even before this streaking vintner made the scene, I was familiar with the eccentric wines traditionally made in Tissot's area, the Arbois. Although only fifty miles southeast from the famed Burgundy vineyards of Domaine de la Romanée-Conti, the Arbois is best known for *vin jaune* (literally "yellow wine"). This sherry-like white couldn't be further from the foresty and mysterious Pinot Noirs and crisp yet full Chardonnays for which Burgundy is famous. Made from a local varietal called Savagnin, vin jaune is created by putting the freshly pressed juice in small barrels that are then left to age. Unlike most wine, which is topped off in the barrel as it evaporates, the barrels containing future vin jaune are left to produce *voiles* ("veils"). This putrid-looking film is what gives the wine its distinctive—and some would say repulsive—taste: nutty and rich but at times disconcertingly similar to that jug of Pinot Grigio you left open a few months ago next to the stove. Even the bottle, a 620-milliliter (ml) flask called a *clavelin* (versus the normal 750-ml bottle used worldwide), screams "Vive la difference!" I can appreciate vin jaune, and I like it in small doses, preferably accompanied by a strong local Jura cheese such as Comté. But I respect this quirky creation more than I enjoy it.

Tissot's family has been in the Arbois for six generations, and one could imagine his weirdness is hardwired. Yet Stephane, mild-mannered, balding, wearing a check shirt and wire-rimmed glasses, didn't look like a kook. When I asked about it, Tissot said that biodynamics was about thinking of the farm as a "living organism." You cannot make great wines, he continued, without great soil. Recently, Stephane contended, there has been an overreliance on using technology to rescue inferior fruit. There are a lot of processes used in winemaking that can boost the flavor ("pumping," by which the newly pressed juice is recirculated in vats to intensify the fermentation process), soften the bitterness ("malolactic fermentation," which breaks down malic acid by adding another fermentation), or, when all else fails, make it as "buttery" as possible to hide a wine's flaws (stick some oak chips in the barrel). Biodynamic winemakers, he explained, eschew chemicals and prefer to work their fields by hand. When he spoke of "crop rotation," "sustainable farming," "cover crops," and "natural yeasts," he had me nodding in agreement. According to the movement's official certifying organization, called Demeter, biodynamic farming produces one of the smallest carbon footprints of any agricultural method.

Biodynamic was starting to sound like organic plus— everything you love about organic and then some. My customers seem to agree. "Even Walmart has organic," one regular pointed out. "Biodynamic," she continued, "is more natural, better." Sure, Tissot's products cost a little more than other dessert wines (a half bottle retails for $47.99), but wasn't it worth it for the greenest wine on the planet? So far so good, I thought.

Tissot's wine was also impressive. His pride, Spirale, is a sweet dessert liqueur. The production is similar to that used to make the traditional *vin passerillé* (literally, "straw wine"): hand-harvested grapes are dried on straw mats for several months, fermented for an entire year, then put in barrels to age for several more. It's hard to argue with the results. Deep, caramelly, and unctuous; you don't have to be a wine snob to want to finish the bottle.

When we polished off the Spirale, I asked Stephane to expound further on the intricacies of the biodynamic way. I think he could see me smirk when he said that he preferred to pick under the full moon (naked, I suspected), but he quickly diffused my suspicion when he explained that the full moon exerts strong gravity on the plants, pulling the water up in the fruit, resulting in plumper "berries" (individual grapes).

Yet it was hard to keep an open mind when he started detailing the making of chamomile sausages out of cows' intestines and their burial at the fall equinox until they have amassed the proper "etheric and astral forces," at which point the goop is disinterred. Likewise, I had to turn away when he described lovingly packing ripe cow dung into a female cow's horns to make a potion that would fertilize a whole field. Yarrow plant stuffed into deer's bladder, dandelions stuffed into bovine peritoneum, and oak bark stuffed more ominously into the skull of a "domesticated animal" rounded out this menu of entrails farci. Could this be, I wondered, just his unpolished English, like bad subtitles in an art house foreign film? Was this a joke?

His practices stem from the theories of Rudolf Steiner, an Austrian philosopher and the founder of biodynamic farming. Steiner is just the kind of Renaissance man I'm inclined to give the benefit of the doubt to: he was a wide-ranging intellectual who founded the well-known Waldorf schools (now an international network of more than a thousand schools), designed seventeen buildings, and wrote more than forty volumes of novels, plays, and poetry. He promoted ethics and civil equality.

Steiner's principles of biodynamism grew out of a series of lectures he gave in 1924 in response to recent crop failures. Biodynamics is based on his belief that there is an objective spiritual world ("anthroposophy") behind farming; it's a philosophy that combines astronomy, biology, and a dollop of mysticism. To farm well, according to Steiner, you not only have to reject industrialized agriculture, you have to acknowledge the Spirits that influence crops. Among them are Gnomes, who live beneath the ground and push plants upward; Undines, who foster budding; Sylphs, who wither mature plants; and Salamanders, fire spirits who imbue seeds with the heat they need to germinate.

More than recycling wastewater, encouraging biodiversity, and avoiding pesticides, the real faith behind biodynamics lies in a series of these preparations designed to spark the "memory of the soil," thereby, Steiner believed, igniting those supernatural "terrestrial and cosmic forces." The preparations are numbered from 500 to 508 (go figure). In addition to the recipes Tissot had mentioned, there are cow horn with cow dung (number 500), cow horn with quartz (number 501), deer bladder with yarrow (number 502), intestines with chamomile (number 503), skull with bark (number 505), and peritoneum with dandelions (number 506). There are also stinging nettle tea (number 504), a sweetly scented herb called valerian (number 507), and horse tail (number 508).

All these concoctions are either applied to the field in minute quantities (grams per acre) or added to compost piles at the appropriate dates on the astrological calendar. Just half a pound of the manure is considered enough to treat two and a half acres of land.

The science behind the catalyzing preparations remains dubious. A Washington State University study points to increased disease resistance as a result of the oak bark, but only in zucchini! Most other blind studies point to increased soil health, but not more than is found in traditional organic farms.

And it gets weirder. Are field mice a problem? Just spread ashes made from burning their skins over the vineyards, but only when Venus is in Scorpio. If weeds are an issue, collect some seeds from the target undesirable plants and incinerate them above a wooden flame that is kindled by the same weeds and then add the residue to the "clear" urine of a sterile cow. Mind you, don't forget to first expose the urine to the full moon for six hours. The aim, according to the Demeter handbook, is to "render the weed infertile by blocking lunar influence."

There seems to be tacit agreement among many biodynamic proponents not to let you know more until you're deemed prepared. Mike Benzinger, founding winemaker of his family's California vineyard, explains this reticence in an article in *San Francisco Weekly*: "One of the things you have to be careful about is overprojecting information to people before they're ready," he says. "Look into history. There have always been initiates, and no one is willing to tell novice secrets about the way the world works. They'd be blown away. You see the face of God, you die, right?"

Extraterrestrials, occult forces, talking mountains, nutty theories withheld until you're "ready": Tissot's winemaking was starting to sound less like science and more like Scientology. Is bio-dynamics, I was starting to wonder, the winemaking equivalent to Dianetics?

Oh, and that bit about the gravity of the full moon? It turns out, according to University of California–Berkeley professor Alex Filippenko, that if a two-pound bunny were to scurry beneath the vine, it would be exerting 750 to 1,000 times the pull of our small satellite.

The only thing a rep likes better than dragging a winemaker to stores is getting one to perform at a winemaker dinner. For the most part, these events are designed to pump customers with enough wine to start them buying case after case. One slick but endearing salesman was the first to propose that we host one in our enoteca. "I sold $10,000 [for the shop owner] at the last one," he boasted. The real carrot, however, was the winemaker, the charismatic Alessandro Mori.

In the heart of Montalcino, Mori's family owns Il Marroneto, a heralded Brunello vineyard. Dashing and talented, Alessandro is exactly the kind of person with whom anyone would want to have dinner. (Imagine George Clooney in the wine business.) Somebody (I hope it was not me) suggested: "Why don't we make a few bistecche alla fiorentina to go with the wine and toss in some salad and a few spears of asparagus gratinée to start?" "Great," we all thought.

The day before the dinner, Janet got the best meat we could from the Greenwich Village butcher Pino's Prime Meats: aged, well-marbled slabs ($500). I drove to Fairway Market in Harlem and bought a wholesale quantity of baby rucola ($85) and four hundred spears of asparagus ($350). Once we got everything back to the store, it was clear that the vintage stove in our apartment was not going to be adequate to make steak for thirty-five, much less all that asparagus. Someone (I truly forget who) suggested that we rent a grill ($160, including delivery) and put it outside in the garden. Janet would man the grill in the back while I boiled and broiled the asparagus upstairs. Several hours later, the grill arrived in pieces and without charcoal. Just as we got it fired up, guests started to arrive.

Alessandro made a series of toasts, starting with his simplest rosso. The good stuff, the verticals (selections of successive vintages) of their flagship wine, would wait until we served the steaks. Despite the late start, all was going perfectly until the thunderstorm. While, five flights up, I was madly trying to broil four hundred asparagus spears a dozen at a time, Janet decided to hang a tarp over the top of the grill pit to keep the rain off the steaks. Smoke quickly billowed through the windows and just as quickly enveloped the room. The smoke alarm went off. The gratinée was charring. Somehow we finished cooking the steaks and saved the asparagus. The wine started flowing: 2001, 1997, 1985! By the end of the evening, amid shots of Alessandro's grappa, guests were exchanging e-mail addresses and promising to see one another again. Arm in arm and in twos and threes, the rest of the group slowly exited amid laughter. One couple lagged, making out in the soggy garden. Alessandro gave me a hug. The experience was an incredible success except that nobody—not one person—bought wine. That memorable dinner, I would discover later, had been totally illegal.

Sometimes winemakers show up without their reps. One afternoon I returned from a portfolio tasting, a seasonal event at which you are jostled about like a kid at a kegger as dozens of your competitors gulp down a distributor's umpteen offerings. I was exhausted and happy to be back but surprised to find a half dozen Frenchmen stiffly sitting in the enoteca sipping a bottle of pricey Côte de Beaune. It turns out that they were all Burgundy producers in for another trade event. In the corner, looking particularly serious, was Armand Rousseau, the maker of the Pinot Noir that had so wowed us on the second floor. Janet was giddy and smiling, oblivious to her purple-stained teeth.

The next morning I was even more stunned to find the same group hanging out in the same spot looking as if they had just taken an all-night train from Bangladesh. Thin-lipped Rousseau was smoking. In my best high school French, I managed to find out that Janet had taken it upon herself to entertain the guys that night. And where does a tattooed twentysomething with purple-stained teeth and lensless Sally Jessy Raphael glasses decide she's going to take a group of France's most esteemed winemakers?

"Zee Ustler [Hustler] Club," murmured one of the monsieurs, a burly Philippe Starck look-alike.

Evidently, Janet had secured a VIP pass (God knows how or why or when) for the establishment where they had spent most of the evening enjoying wine, women, and song. Janet, I later discovered from Armando, had attended personally to Mr. Rousseau.

Yet the all-nighter only amped her enthusiasm. For the next several weeks, Janet attacked selling with vigor. On more than one occasion, I remember having to calm her down after she whooped over the sale of a bottle of Châteauneuf-du-Pape. Becky and I were simultaneously horrified and in awe.

By the summer of 2005, we certainly were selling a lot of wine at the shop. I tried to overlook the fact that Janet rarely made it to work in time to open at ten o'clock. She was still going to portfolio tastings only to return several hours later with those purple teeth.

One day, things came to a head when Janet took it upon herself to change the store hours. Sundays, she decided, we would close early. It did not matter what the gilded lettering on the door said or what we had listed on our website or what we had filed with the State Liquor Authority. Janet thought 5 p.m. was just fine.

Feeling like the parents of a rebellious teenager, Becky and I reminded her of our obligations as a retailer. A store, we told her, must be reliable. Instead of closing early, we suggested, let's get you some help.

Janet replied that she needed no one else. An Italian (boy) friend with a basement wineshop in the East Village told her that he did everything himself. Why couldn't she?

A few weeks later, Janet changed her mind. She told us that she had discovered just the right person to join the staff: Mariko, an Italian wine connoisseur who worked the floor of a famous wineshop just to be in close proximity to her passion. After meeting Mariko, Becky had her doubts. I told her not to worry. Almost immediately, we realized we (I) had screwed up once again. Respectful to the point of dour, Mariko meted out every taste of Chianti as if it were part of a tea ceremony but could not relate to customers who didn't recognize the transcendence that is an Aldo Conterno Barolo. We were in a bind. We had just negotiated a contract with a mature adult and were loath to just turn around and let her go. But Janet was as adamant about her dismissal as she had been about her hiring: "I can't work with that . . . prig!" "Fire her!" she kept demanding. And, eventually, we did.

During the summer lull, when loyal wine buyers seem to abandon the city, we retreated to Cannizzaro for what we hoped would be a welcome dose of carefree Italian life. All we wanted to do was eat and nap. Then I got a call from Cristina, a college classmate and old friend, who asked if we would take the time to visit her childhood friend who had recently bought a vineyard over the ridge from us. We could not say no.

It didn't look promising. As we drove in the hills above Lucca to visit the Tenuta di Valgiano, ten miles north of this Tuscan city, a heat haze looking a lot like smog hung over the walled city. Worse, the baking sun, perfect for growing the olives for which the area is famous, can overripen grapes, resulting in flabby, characterless wines. But since Laura Collobiano, Cristina's pal and a biodynamic maker, had invited us to tour her renovated vineyard, I felt obligated at least to check it out. In addition to my memories of Tissot, the loopy Frenchman, I had good reason to be wary. Lucca is well known for many things (the Roman forum, the medieval main street, the Renaissance ramparts, the olive oil), but not for wine.

Growing up, I was familiar with the local, rather forgettable Montecarlo white (named after the picturesque hill town approximately ten miles west of the city). It was the kind of slightly grape juice-y quencher, light and easy, that's perfect with lunch on a hot summer day. But take away the homemade gnocchi, the pergola, and the rolling vistas and it's hardly worth exporting. (VitaminWater flavors are more memorable.)

Sixteen hairpin turns later, as we zigzagged up the mountainside and emerged from the low-lying haze into the courtyard of a stately sixteenth-century villa, I started to reconsider. Lucca's best villas encircle the valley of the walled city at the same altitude, about 250 meters above sea level. Most are also nestled near ravines cut by mountain streams. The result is a Goldilocks microclimate, neither too hot nor too cold, too sunny or too shady. Perhaps Laura was on to something.

If you think organic means hippy-dippy, you've never met Laura (Avogadro dei Conti di Valdengo e) Collobiano, the vineyard's proprietor, along with her husband Moreno. Laura, winner of the prestigious journal *Gambero Rosso*'s "Organic Winemaker of the Year" in 2008, favors an androgynous uniform of man's jacket over jeans and sturdy boots. She operates her vineyard with a demanding intensity. I certainly didn't have to worry about her prancing naked through the fields.

As we walked down the rejuvenated main street that runs along the service part of the estate, Laura spoke of her mission to revitalize the whole forty-acre farm. Unlike the wealthy English who've long taken refuge in Lucca's estates, Laura's focus was not just on cosmetic restoration but also on rejuvenation of the entire system on which these estates originally operated: a self-sustaining farm with livestock and vegetables. This was the fattoria reborn.

We'd arrived in the middle of bottling, and the vineyard was abuzz. In an open graveled area, a specially outfitted truck filled, corked, capped, and labeled the wines in one shot. As the truck spewed diesel exhaust, the clatter was deafening, and to my relief, as far as I could see, no one was chanting or strewing crystals. Far from the churning assembly line, lunch was a familiar exercise in studied informality. We sat in the kitchen, but the kitchen

was monumental: sixteen-foot ceilings, massive cast iron cook-
ers topped with bubbling pots attended by uniformed women
in aprons. In front of the table were glass doors opening up to a
graveled terrace dotted with potted lemon trees, framed by stone
railings, and looking out toward olive tree–covered mountains
beyond.

The menu was deceptively simple: spaghetti ai frutti di mare,
a seafood pasta. Only later did Laura (whose equally fastidious
uncle was Giovanni Agnelli, the legendary scion of the Fiat family) reveal that the fish had been bought directly from a fisherman
in Viareggio and that the pasta had been brought from a favored
supplier in Naples. No wonder she finds the rigors of biodynamism so appealing. With its prescription-size preparations and
demanding schedule, biodynamic farming seems tailor-made for
obsessives; no Type A wants just to sit and watch grapes grow.

As Laura uncorked the first bottle of her basic Tenuta di
Valgiano red, I was wondering whether I'd be able to taste the
benefits of all this attention to detail. As I swirled the glass, the
first sniff was promising. The wine smelled like a bowl of ripe
fruit, without any obvious defects. No sawdusty wood odors, no
sinus-clearing alcoholic bite, no whiff of decay. Just a big bunch
of plump grapes. The taste was also full, velvety, and brimming
with fruit essence.

In truth, it was hard to tell if some of this clarity was due
to the cow's horn or just to good organic farming. Or was that
purity a result of some other aspect of Laura's demanding regi-
men? At Valgiano, for example, the grapes are crushed within
three hours of picking. Could the wine's pure taste actually be the
result of the quick processing of the picked bunches?

Over lunch, Laura espoused passions similar to those of Monsieur Tissot, but she emphasized the natural over the mystical. It was as if they had entirely different readings of the same religious text. Her focus was more on responsible agriculture than on supernatural viscera: crop rotations to build the soil and butterflies to eat pesky aphids. I was familiar with stinging nettles, having stepped on my share as a kid. If you brush up against *ortica*, as it's known in Tuscan dialect, you won't want to touch it again. I could see why a bug wouldn't either. Despite the exotic recipes, a lot of these preparations come down to the use of rotting organic matter. And even I know that compost seems to be good for almost everything you'd want to grow. Much of the other practices (e.g., no pesticides, no hormones) fall into the mainstream of sensible organic agriculture.

Laura was considerably more dogmatic on one common winemaking technique that has nothing to do with biodynamism: mixing grapes. Europeans traditionally have blended varietals, whereas we Americans tend to be grape-fixated. We want pure Chardonnays and pure Pinot Noirs; they combine varietals to improve wines. Purity, Laura reminded me, doesn't mean sticking to one grape. In Valgiano's case, Sangiovese, the foundation of the most revered Tuscan wine, Brunello di Montalcino, can be tannic (as in mouth-puckering) when young. To offset its bite, Laura adds round and mellow Merlot as well as rich Syrah. The result is a wine that will age well (those tannins soften over the years) and has a deep lingering taste without the harshness of pure Sangiovese.

Harder to swallow was her contention, one that she shares with many of her biodynamic colleagues, that her wines have more *terroir*, or "sense of place," than those farmed by conventional methods. The idea sounds so good: Who wouldn't want to have more local character in an increasingly global and homogenized world? The trouble is that whereas Laura grows the types of grapes that are on her plot of land (Sangiovese, Merlot, Syrah, and, for her white wines, Malvasia, Trebbiano, and Vermentino), no one else nearby makes the same blend. It's not like going to Saint-Émilion in France, where winemakers traditionally have adhered to a specific ratio of grapes (70 percent Merlot, 15 percent Cabernet Franc, and 15 percent Cabernet Sauvignon). Crack open a Premier Cru, right-bank Bordeaux and even a slightly tutored neophyte can identify it. This is not the case in Lucca's foothills. Laura's wine may taste like her patch of earth or not, but there isn't much basis for comparison or a tradition of making that particular blend. Indeed, red wines of similar richness and depth are now found throughout the world. Her fresh and full wines, the products of cutting-edge techniques, arguably tell you more about when they were made than where. After our meal, we emerged from an ancient tunnel under the villa to continue our discussion. I got the feeling that Laura, like many biodynamic winemakers, treats the astrological part of Steiner's theories the way we treat horoscopes. It's not that I fear Mercury in retrograde, but just in case, I'm not going to push it either.

Other winemakers are harder to read. Certainly, most acknowledge that biodynamics has become shorthand for "I care more about my vineyard" and therefore a powerful marketing tool. Tyler Colman, an acquaintance and the writer of the popular *Dr. Vino* blog, described a conversation he had with a well-known Napa vintner. Even though the winemaker wasn't a true believer, he switched his vineyard to biodynamic farming

FRIED SAGE LEAVES

SERVES 8

When friends come over, I like to whip up a batch of these salty treats to serve with cocktails while I am cooking. The batch I made for our first holiday party disappeared even more quickly than the Prosecco.

¼ CUP ALL-PURPOSE FLOUR

2 CUPS OLIVE OIL

2 EGGS, BEATEN

50 LARGE FRESH SAGE LEAVES,
RINSED AND PATTED DRY

SEA SALT TO TASTE

Pour the flour onto a plate. Set aside. In a medium skillet, heat ¼ inch of the oil over medium-high heat until it starts to ripple. Holding each sage leaf by its stem, dip it in the egg, then toss the leaf in the flour. Shake the leaf to remove the extra flour. Add each leaf to the oil and then remove the leaves in the order in which they were added. Aim for one big batch at a time. Fry 30 seconds per side. Drain on paper towels and sprinkle with the sea salt. Serve with aperitivi.

For a fancier, more uniform coating, my friend makes a beer batter variation:

2 CUPS ALL-PURPOSE FLOUR

½ CUP BEER (I LIKE PIEDMONT'S MENABREA, BUT ANY PILSNER WILL DO)

1 CUP SELTZER WATER

2 EGGS, SEPARATED

PINCH OF SALT

50 LARGE FRESH SAGE LEAVES, RINSED AND PATTED DRY

In a mixing bowl, whisk together the flour, beer, seltzer, and egg yolks until the mixture is the consistency of heavy cream. In a separate medium bowl, whisk the egg whites with a pinch of salt until they form stiff peaks. Fold the egg whites into the beer batter with a rubber spatula.

Holding each leaf by its stem, dip it into the beer batter. Gently shake off excess batter. Add each leaf to the oil, and then remove the leaves in the order in which they were added. Aim for one big batch at a time. Fry 30 seconds per side. Drain on paper towels and sprinkle with salt. Serve with aperitivi.

because, he said, "at his price point, everything is extremely competitive, and he didn't want to allow his competitors who were practicing biodynamics to have any sort of an advantage."

What is clear is that biodynamic farmers tend to be skilled and successful, able to trade lower yields for higher prices. And although there's no direct correlation between biodynamism and wine quality, biodynamic wines do tend to taste better than their more conventionally made counterparts. They also include some of the most experienced and esteemed names in the business: Nicolas Joly, Leroy, Zind-Humbrecht, Weinbach, Deiss, Chapoutier, Gravner, Domaine Leflaive, Alvaro Palacios, and some Domaine de la Romanée-Conti (the scarcest, most expensive, and, frequently, best wine in the world). No one can accuse these guys of being loopy. Savvy? Yes. Cynical? Maybe. Nutty? Not a chance. One thing was for sure: biodynamic wine would definitely have a place in our store.

It's hard not to be seduced by the romance of winemaking, which is fine for someone splurging on something to sip with his risotto but dangerous for a wineshop owner. You can do a lot of crazy things for love, and getting stuck with fifty cases of expensive and incredibly well-made wine that won't be drinkable for another five years is one of them. My livelihood depends on keeping enchantment in check.

Despite the temptations, our shop was making money as we ended our first year. The problem was that the building renovation demanded more cash than the store—and our savings—could supply. After a year of celebration, I suspected a hangover was coming at the end of 2006. But I was determined to end the year as festively as we had begun it.

For our first Christmas party, we created a live nativity scene.

The store was strewn with hay, and we set up a tented manger in the enoteca that featured a Nebuchadnezzar (equivalent to twenty regular-size bottles) of Bellenda ("Bethlehem" Prosecco) in the cradle. We dressed in diaphanous white robes. With his curly blond locks, Luca would have looked better in the cradle, but try getting an eighteen-month-old toddler to sit still. We even borrowed a real camel from the holiday show at Radio City Music Hall.

Our place was packed. The camel was stationed in front of the store. Outside, I could read the lips of passing drivers as they mouthed, "Oh, my God." Soon, a small crowd blocked the entrance and cameras were flashing just like at a movie premiere. The year-end bash felt like a bookend to our opening party as once again the store was filled with smiling neighbors, customers, and friends.

That is, until I saw who Janet was kissing in the back corner of the enoteca. "This," I thought, "could change everything."

chapter 4

CRUSH

MESSY AND SATISFYING, the crush is fun. Generally.

The goal is not so much to obliterate the berries as to squish them gently to burst their skins and release their juice. First, bunches fresh from the harvest are sorted on big tables. After removing twigs, bugs, and moldy fruit, the workers put the grapes in enormous vats. To keep from pulverizing the bitter seeds along with the pulp, many of our producers still hand (or, more accurately, foot) crush their fruit just as Lucille Ball did on *I Love Lucy*. One Tuscan vintner favors young coeds in bikinis to trample his grapes.

Beneath the frolicking among the pulp, the crush is a turning point. So far, the grape has been babied as it has grown from bud to fruit; now it's obliterated. Man takes over from nature. Chemistry trumps agriculture. Winemakers may rejoice at the tangible first step of winemaking, but their levity is short-lived. New hurdles are on the horizon. You'd better watch your barrel.

N OUR SECOND YEAR OF BUSINESS, like Luca, who was just learning to walk, I found myself excited but stumbling and occasionally hitting my head. It started with the reps.

Armando called to see if he could swing by to show me "things that would sell themselves." Out of his bag, he pulled a half dozen bargain Australian wines. They had names like Snake Charmer, Strait Jacket, and Cycle Buff Beauty. Most were Shiraz-based blends, for which Australia is well known. We weren't exactly encouraged by his focus on the labels. "Isn't that fun?" he said, gesturing at a bottle that featured an illustration of a bikini-clad woman running away while screaming. The rest of the labels looked to have been inspired by the animated television series *South Park*. Sitting on one side of the table, Janet, Becky, and I were suspicious but trying to keep open minds. Australia makes some fantastic wines. So what if many of their vineyards also favor bad graphic design and have a tendency to overbrand?

Armando's selections were uniformly syrupy goop. Becky detected "hints of wood shavings." None were much like any of the wines we had tasted in over a year of business. It's not that they were undrinkable; it's that they didn't taste like what we had grown to expect wine to taste like. These were more like smoothies with a kick.

"Can you taste the fruit?" Armando asked eagerly.

"Hmm." I nodded and waited for some sign that would help me understand why he had just shown us this lineup. After a few uncomfortable seconds, I jumped in: "Thanks! Really interesting selection. We'll get back to you."

Armando was hardly out the door before Becky asked, "Was

that for real?" Janet was confused. Did this former sommelier
not recognize that these wines were crummy? Did Armando
truly feel that these wines would sell even if they were not to our
tastes? Or was he just trying to unload a few dogs in his portfolio
that he was nonetheless obligated to hawk with the same conviction with which he sold his Châteauneuf-du-Pape?

Could I really trust the guy I'd spied locking lips with my
manager at our holiday party?

Over the next weeks what became clear is that Armando was
not the only salesman pushing his "value" wines. At the same
time, we were finding it harder to source some of the gems we
had stocked the previous year. The rare Tuscan red Cerbaiona?
"Sold out." The equally coveted Turley Zinfandel? "Out of stock."

Even Southern was no help. Lovable Matt was promoted. In
his stead appeared Joe, a younger guy in a similarly baggy suit
who pecked away at a ThinkPad. Joe did not make custom guitars, and neither did he open a pipeline to the good stuff. But he
sure knew the SKU (short for "stock-keeping unit," retail-speak
for a product's unique identifying number) of our bestselling
budget white, La Poule Blanche ("The White Chicken"). "Five-case drop?" he'd ask as he stared into the computer screen.

Although no distributor actually came out and said it, I was
starting to realize that there was a quid pro quo: help me unload
some of the thirty thousand no-name bottles I have sitting in
a container in Port Elizabeth, New Jersey, and I'll help you get
the coveted brands, the 100-point wines, and whatever else sells
itself. Each rep, we later found out, had an allocation of gems he
could dole out to his best customers. Now that we were no longer
new enough to merit special incentives, we were constrained to
buy wines that, though good, would require the dreaded "hand

sell." The hand sell, the one-on-one explanation required to get a consumer familiar with an obscure bottle, frightens big stores looking for fast turnover. Not that we minded explaining over and over again the virtues of Quincy (a little known appellation next to Sancerre that offers the same crisp Sauvignon Blanc at half the price), but we did not want to be shut out from the collectible fare.

Janet suggested that we investigate the "gray" market. She knew people. We would just have to leap as soon as the offers presented themselves. The gray market is a shadowy and loose collection of brokers and hustlers who are not the original importers of the wine they sell. At best, buying wine from one of these sources is like acquiring a painting from a secondary art dealer. More often, buying wine from a guy named Eddie feels like picking up a used car. The pitch hardly varies: somehow (almost always, we are told, it came from a "finicky" collector who wanted to "prune" his collection), he got a hold of a cache of 1989 Lafite Rothschild. With wine, particularly champagne, gray marketers can buy at retail in Europe, bring it to the United States, and still sell it at a profit. Although it is possible that this wine had been lovingly pampered in a temperature-controlled cellar, it's also conceivable that those bottles had baked for the last ten years in a Hong Kong shop window. Did I really want to take the chance?

There are some retailers who do. One particularly notorious shop on the Upper East Side is known to be able to scrounge up a few cases of 1961 Pomerol with a phone call or two. The two partners also have been linked to Hardy Rodenstock, the now infamous German collector who allegedly faked the world's most expensive wine, a claret reputedly owned by Thomas Jefferson. (The purported fraud was detailed in Benjamin Wallace's book *The Billionaire's Vinegar*.) There's a lot of cash to be made from get-me-that-at-whatever-cost transactions. Although avarice seems to be the primary motivation for these shady deals, a desire for intrigue also seems to fuel their desire. Secret sales with dicey middlemen are sexy. Tellingly, one of the partners in this particular shop also has had great success distributing the wine of his ex-wife, a famous porn actress. She is naked on the label. Robert Parker gave her wine 90 points.

Although some of these gray market offers were tempting— 80 percent off La Tâche!—we turned them all down, much to Janet's dismay. Sure, we could make a few bucks, but not without two terrifying risks: first, the authorized importer of those goods certainly will not appreciate your thriftiness. Try buying something else from Southern, for example, if they catch you buying Gaja from a wineshop in Florence. Second, your customer may end up screaming mad at you for unwittingly selling spoiled wine.

In the worst case, the wine you buy isn't just poorly stored, it's completely fake. Everyone seems to know someone who's been had. I recall reading about a broker, Everett Love, who was burned by a gray market purchase of fraudulent wine. In 2007, he bought six bottles of 1982 Château Lafite Rothschild from a Los Angeles broker, who'd in turn bought it from a broker in the Bay Area. Love sent the wine directly to a client in China. The client found a loose capsule on a bottle and discovered the cork was stamped 1981, a vintage that sells for a quarter of the price of the 1982. Last I heard, Love was irate and still trying to get back his money.

My nixing of the pursuit of the gray market irritated Janet. More and more, she was slinking in with dry lips and hooded eyes. After one particularly rough binge, our wine director decided to do a master cleanse, and for ten days she swore off drinking. In place of food and wine, Janet sipped water spiked with cayenne pepper and maple syrup. Her mood faltered. More long nights followed. She tried another cleanse. And another. While fasting, Janet no longer let out loose whoops over sales of $150 Cabernets. She just looked unhappy. One day I bought her a spa treatment and told her to take off the afternoon. The next day she complained about the pedicure.

She needed a break. We did, too. As a bonus for her holiday dedication (and a little breather for Becky and myself), we gave Janet a round-trip ticket trip to her favorite place in the whole world: Burgundy. But Janet never made it back on the return flight. Her cell phone was off. Two days after she was supposed to have been back at work, I got a cryptic message that said our Pinot Noir–loving manager would be back in another two weeks: "There was work to do."

I wanted to hide her maple syrup. I wanted to break those red glasses. I wanted to let her go. But we were afraid. Given our headaches in finding good people, what was I going to do in the interim? Suddenly become the wine buyer/manager?

The low point was the day I came upon Janet crying at the cash register. The night before, she confessed, she had had a terrible fight with Jude. They had both been drunk. Jude was history.

Meanwhile, Jude's career was taking off. He was promoted to head of operations. The auction business, arguably the most legitimate gray market source, was skyrocketing. What had been a $5 million a year business when I attended that auction at Cru in 2005 had ballooned to $80 million by 2010. The venerable Upper West Side Manhattan shop found its substantial $5 million annual retail sales dwarfed by its auction revenues as it became the world's largest fine wine auctioneer. And all this out of an unassuming storefront sandwiched between a Jamba Juice and a Foot Locker.

Jude attributes part of their success to luring sellers with no premium (while whacking buyers with a 22 percent surcharge). But the most compelling reason for the store's growth can be summed up in one word: China. Jude quickly recognized that the gravitational center of wine was shifting from London and New York to Hong Kong. The "Las Vegas of wine," Jude calls it. Flush with cash, these buyers were aching to spend it on big-ticket bottles.

Jude was, and remains, the perfect guy for the job. As lieutenant to the chairman, he got front-row access to the persuasive powers of this legendary bon vivant. According to Jude, the pot-smoking wine expert relishes late nights with clients, dishing inside stories at famous wineries as they toss back magnums of 1921 Cheval Blanc.

What set Jude ahead of his slightly stuffy competitors is that he was an outsider too, albeit one with his nose pressed firmly against the glass. He summered out east, but in down-market Hampton Bays. His father is in "banking of some sort," Jude told me over lunch, but, it turns out, in the information technology division. Conversant with the inside but not a part of it, he can straddle the fence as both an Etonesque wine purveyor and an enthusiastic enabler of the Chinese nouveau riche.

Boy, does he enable. Recently, Jude hosted a dinner for forty-five atop the Great Wall for their best clients. According to Jude, clients were encouraged to invite their entourages. One guy brought fifteen of his closest friends on the auction house's dime.

For the Far Eastern buyer, Jude contends, wine is the "ultimate showy display of wealth." It's an expensive object whose worth evaporates once you pop the cork.

While Jude was busy jet-setting to Hong Kong, we thought we might try to capture a shard of the high-end market. Thanks to a generous friend and collector, we put aside some money to focus on high-end Burgundy. Why kill ourselves over small sales, we figured, when we could make that and more by snaring a few connoisseurs with whom Janet was already going out to dinner?

What we did not realize is that patrician billionaires and other carriage trade mainstays were no longer the epicenter of the wine world. In contrast to the 1970s, when a pioneering cluster of baby boomers spearheaded wine consumption, around 13 percent of American drinkers now consume 87 percent of all wine. The newest generation of oenophiles is more affluent than filthy rich and more suburban than urban. The self-made billionaires and Eastern oligarchs who dominate the Chinese market are marginal in the United States.

Here, collectors, foodies, and geeks make up this new trinity of the wine-obsessed. In the New York area, for example, an ex-hippie from New Paltz is one of the largest French wine buyers. Balding with a ponytail, he had been one of the big fish seated at my table during that first auction at Cru, at which I watched him scoop up cases of Montrachet. For every William Koch (the mining heir famous for having bought the world's most expensive wine, a $155,000 bottle reputedly from Thomas Jefferson's cellar that turned out to be fake), there are thousands of guys like the Woodstock bigwig.

In this changed landscape, collectors still nod toward the ratings bestowed by Robert Parker, the lawyer turned wine critic and publisher of *Wine Advocate,* but they are more likely to trust other sources, such as *Dr. Vino,* winner of Best American Wine Blog award of 2007 and one of the wine world's most popular bloggers. We were learning that if you want to sell wine to serious collectors, the blessing of *Dr. Vino* was worth more than a 90-point shrug from *Wine Spectator. Dr. Vino* is written by Tyler Colman, a Westchester-based stay-at-home dad. He's the spectacled guy down the street whom you spy typing away at his Mac into the wee hours. When Tyler came to our store to do a book signing, I was struck by how much this lanky, soft-spoken guy matched my preconception of the lone blogger who is most comfortable with a keyboard in front of him and a glass of wine by his side.

Perhaps the most influential critic is neither a publisher nor a blogger but a retailer. In the last five years, Gary Vaynerchuk has transformed his father's Springfield, New Jersey, liquor store, the Wine Library, into a $60 million business. The juggernaut has been fueled by Vaynerchuk's daily webcasts featuring his untraditional takes on wines and the wine industry.

From his first videos in 2006, we were transfixed by the fast-talking Vaynerchuk, who described wines as tasting like Tootsie Rolls and "New York City garbage." Oblivious to the cruddy lighting and bad camera angles, the chunky Jets fan (Vaynerchuk sometimes wears a team jersey during his reviews) thundered, describing one bottle as a "pile of stinky clothes [left] in a college dorm room infested by loose hamsters." In the background, phones ring, but Vaynerchuk insists that his videos are shot in one take.

As refreshingly unself-conscious as he is wildly effusive, Vaynerchuk is a maniac, but one who tells the truth as he sees it.

In fact, he claims to have panned 70 percent of the wines sold in his store. I can't say we always agree on his assessments, nor do I always understand his colorful descriptions. I don't get his significance, but it is clear to everyone at the store that Vaynerchuk is an American original, even if he was born in Babruysk, Belarus.

Vaynerchuk has become a phenomenon, having appeared on *Ellen* and *The Tonight Show with Conan O'Brien*. As Eric Asimov reported in the *New York Times*, "in the guise of educating the host's palate to wine terms like sweaty, mineral, and earthy, he sniffed Mr. O'Brien's armpit and persuaded him to chew an old sock, lick a rock, and eat dirt (topped with shredded cigar tobacco and cherries)." Articles have followed in the *Wall Street Journal*, *GQ*, and *Slate*, where Vaynerchuk was described as the "first wine guru of the YouTube era."

Despite his tens of thousands of website viewers and Facebook friends and nearly a million Twitter followers, Gary claims that the webcasts did little to help Internet sales of wine, which rose only 3 percent. However, phone sales shot up 40 percent in the first year. Vaynerchuk wasn't selling wine, he was selling himself. His strength wasn't so much his Facebook savvy or his Twitter patter as his ability to use those tools to build trust and human relationships. Built up through new media, that trust then sold wine through one-hundred-year-old telephone lines.

At the time, we were oblivious to such subtleties. We equated "Internet" with "money machine." Build a website, I assumed, and they will come. Hence we focused on slapping up a pretty website as soon and as inexpensively as we could. I bought an e-commerce software package from a Russian company and hired a chain-smoking Frenchman (a reclusive customer) to configure it. I will spare you, dear reader, the results of this misguided

United Nations' experiment in digital design. Suffice it to say that it would have been a lot easier to pay a little more and actually have face-to-face meetings with our web developers. Yet after nine months, the website was complete. We even got a few online sales that first year.

We probably should have been blogging, but I was intimidated. As someone besieged by semiexperts in many media, I felt that a daily blog had to have something important to say every day. It had to be smart, and it had to be regular. To take on that platform, I needed more time. Partly, I have to admit, I was not keen on broadcasting my big nose and receding hairline. And given her volatile history, providing Janet with such a soapbox would have made me nervous. For the moment, we were content to watch and learn more about how the wine world really worked.

What we came to realize is that no tweet, Facebook post, e-mail push, or any other clever marketing trick can undo the damage of a cold drizzle. Conversely, a sunny day is every bees-to-honey cliché. For our wine sales, the weather is mightier than the Internet.

In aiming for the big fish, not only did we fail to identify this new generation of influencers and connoisseurs, we also neglected to realize that this high-stakes game of collectible wine sales meant lower margins on larger cash outlays. Unlike most of us, ultracollectors tend to look for very specific wines: the right producer from a particular vineyard in the most desirable vintage. Often finance types, they're used to scanning screens and making decisions that are based on tiny numeric variations. An insular group with established relationships, they also seemed to create their own markets, bidding one supplier against another for the best price. Something we could buy at $100, we would see selling for $110. If we waited ten years, we probably could move that bottle for $200. In the interim, it was a lot cheaper to make that same $10 by buying a $15 wine and selling it for $25.

How, I wondered, did the big guys make their money? The nation's largest wine purveyor, I discovered, was Costco. In 2008, the cut-rate retailer sold seventy-five million bottles for a total of $1.1 billion in sales. Equally surprising is what it sells. Costco moves more Dom Pérignon (125,000 bottles in 2006) than any other store chain in the country. The bargain giant is also the nation's biggest seller of classified-growth French wines, including prestigious names such as Chateau Margaux and Chateau Mouton Rothschild. Last time I looked, you could even pick up a twelve-bottle collection of Chateau d'Yquem, the vaunted French Sauternes, for $5,000.

Costco's customers spend so much ($108 per purchase on average) because they make a lot. According to the company, the average income of its members is almost twice that of the average American household ($74,000 to $47,000) with close to a third pulling in over $100,000 per year. These well-to-do customers don't think twice about plunking a $119 bottle of Dom (regular retail around $175) in the cart next to the two-gallon jugs of extra-virgin olive oil. Costco understands that everyone, including the affluent, loves a bargain.

These blue-chip brand names also set the stage for the inclusion of less known and less expensive selections. "People in the wine industry kind of look down their noses at selling wine at Costco, but we like being tucked between Dom Pérignon and Opus One," says George Rose of Kendall-Jackson, the large California winery.

The real cash cow, however, has been Costco's private blends. Markups on their Kirkland Signature wines are almost double what they get from more traditional brand names. In 2006, Costco sold 130,000 cases of its house label alcoholic beverages. If only we at Pasanella & Son could put together enough cash to buy containers of wine at a time and unravel the myriad federal, state, and local regulations regarding shipping, importing, labeling, and distribution.

We turned to another strategy. At industry events, we heard many colleagues brag about having bought wine "on the D.I." D.I., or direct importing, means that the guy who brought the wine into the country was the person who distributed it. Bargains were supposed to abound because of the elimination of a middleman. What we found is that there were great deals—on one hundred cases. Otherwise, the importer/distributors seemed all too happy to keep a little extra profit for themselves.

Luckily, our tastings business was skyrocketing. Goldman Sachs, Deutsche Bank, and Credit Suisse were booking private tastings in our enoteca. Since Janet was on the verge of a breakdown, the real challenge became getting her help. We thought she would lead the actual tastings. The negotiation, planning, sales, setup, and knockdown would be taken care of by a not-yet-hired miracle worker. That left the door open for almost anybody. Or almost no one.

We were flooded with interest. There was a doctor looking for some part-time work (that a medical professional had extra time should have tipped us off). There was a polite-sounding young man who later sent a thank-you using the e-mail address "moneypiggy." There were actress/sommeliers who sent in head shots. There were slews of guys named Ralph with experience in "likka" stores.

One of our biggest forehead-slapping surprises was that people who work in the wine business like to drink. "Duh!" as even Luca knew to say by then. Two of our most experienced applicants, both of whom had managed multimillion-dollar stores, turned out to have serious problems. One was sued by a previous employer for having drunk—or stashed, or both—$150,000 of inventory. The other had been arrested for driving while intoxicated.

One of our first hires was John Lahart, a retired advertising executive and wine collector. He was interested in working a few evenings a week to learn about wine from "another perspective." We were stunned that someone so accomplished and so qualified would want to sit behind a cash register! From the start, John was a hit with the customers. He was attentive but carefree in the way you are when you do something just for fun. Wine geeks esteemed his knowledge, which spanned California producers that had been famous in the 1970s to the latest cult wine from Bolgheri in Tuscany. Newbies appreciated that our easygoing "floorman" never tried to hustle them into buying expensive bottles. Everyone seemed to enjoy a few minutes of chatting with jolly John.

We still needed full-time help, particularly with our events.

In walked Suzanne, a recent San Diego State graduate with no wine experience. But Becky had a hunch that she would be perfect, and she was right. Suzanne was dedicated, smart, responsible, and endlessly patient. She had a sincere interest in wine (and has since received a master's in wine marketing from Milan's Bocconi School of Management, aka "Italy's Wharton," and now works as wine director of New York's Alta restaurant). Best of all, under her sweet exterior, Suzanne is actually sweet.

During Suzanne's tenure, our private events took off. From Dog the Bounty Hunter to Caroline Kennedy (who came to the same event hosted by their publisher), all sorts of notables waded through the fish guts and deserted streets to find us.

That September, we got a call to arrange a tasting for the British chef Nigella Lawson, who turned out to be as gracious as she is gorgeous. Two months later, we heard from one of her countrymen and fellow chefs: Jamie Oliver was looking for a place to have a dinner to celebrate the publication of his wife Jools's book *Diary of an Honest Mum*.

Becky and I had met Jamie in 2000 when a friend had called with a tempting proposition: How would you like to have a soon-to-be famous chef make you and your friends dinner? The only catch was that the meal would have to be photographed for *Food & Wine* magazine. As the date approached, we got a call. "Would you mind," a publicist asked, "if we could add a few of Jamie's [read: more photogenic] pals?" "Sure, no problem," I told her. The day before we received another query: "So sorry to bother you," the publicist apologized, "but do you think we could move the dinner a little earlier, to, say, four-thirty?" "Oh, and don't worry," she added mysteriously, "the food will be real."

Despite some missing friends, the late afternoon pasta party turned out to be one of the more memorable meals we ever had in our Meatpacking District loft. Initially, I was touched by how nervous Jamie was to cook for us "Italians." By the end, Jamie was happily perched on our Vespa, which we stored in our loft, while munching away on pasta with cauliflower. The food was delicious, if not exactly piping hot—the photographer had instructed us not to chew while we were being shot.

We were feeling the pressure of being tasked with supplying

JAMIE OLIVER'S
ROASTED PARSNIPS
SERVES 6

To celebrate the publication of his first book, Jamie Oliver made us dinner in our old Meatpacking District loft. Several years before we opened the wineshop, Jamie taught me a recipe for roasted parsnips that I now make about once a month. He paired the vegetables with roast lamb, as I often do.

18 PARSNIPS

1 HEAD OF GARLIC

3 SPRIGS OF FRESH ROSEMARY

OLIVE OIL

SEA SALT AND FRESHLY GROUND BLACK PEPPER

Preheat the oven to 400°F. Peel the parsnips and quarter them lengthways. Break the garlic head into cloves, leaving them unpeeled, and smash them slightly with the side of a chef's knife or cleaver. Pick the rosemary leaves from the woody stalks.

Add a few generous "lugs," as Jamie calls them, of olive oil to a large roasting pan. Toss in the garlic and rosemary leaves. Put the parsnips into the pan with a good pinch of salt and pepper and stir them around to coat them in the flavors. Spread out the parsnips evenly into one layer—this is important, because you want them to roast, not steam, as they will if they are on top of each other. Roast the parsnips in the preheated oven for about 1 hour, or until golden and crisp.

the food and wine for Jools's dinner. Thank goodness, we had some Italian friends with a nearby restaurant who were willing to take on the job. As they shuttled from the restaurant kitchen bearing steaming platters of gnocchi and homemade tordelli, we opened a selection of offbeat southern Italian wines. I still remember Jaime's favorite, a Ciavolich Aries Pecorino from the Abruzzi region. A white wine with a pronounced herbal quality; we nicknamed it the "pot" wine. He called it "wicked!"

One of the most fun events we created took place in an abandoned train tunnel. Our installation for a design industry AIDS benefit featured a table surrounded by walls made of racks of drying spaghetti and a ceiling hung with 148 grape bunches. The last-minute addition of a male public relations intern who was persuaded to crush grapes with his feet in a barrel while dressed as Lucille Ball (kerchief, gingham blouse, pedal pushers) made it a hit. We were on a roll.

Of course, we also had our share of duds. I was very excited about a grappa tasting combined with a card lesson. By 1 a.m., we'd emptied six bottles (almost $500 worth) and the group was just getting warmed up—except for one slight young woman who passed out. Sip 'n' Cinema, our weekly free tasting and movie, was similarly hit or miss. One time it coincided with game four of the World Series. *Dead Calm* was exactly that. One person came.

Yet that second year was not spent entirely spitting with sales reps in the back of the store. When Becky and I went to Italy again in the summer of 2007 to visit my father and Lisetta, we felt we could not turn down an invitation to a nearby lunch organized by a consortium of wine producers in southern Tuscany's Maremma region. For centuries, this coastal territory remained

unspoiled and sparsely populated as its low-lying marshland harbored malaria. In the 1930s, Mussolini filled in the swamps as
part of a huge land reclamation project called the Agro Pontino.
Although the region remains one of the least recognized areas
of one of the world's most popular tourist destinations, insiders
are familiar with its pristine vistas, Italian cowboys, and, imagine
this, rodeos. No wonder Sergio Leone shot his Westerns in the
Maremma.

During the 1980s, the Marchese Antinori, who had vineyards
in neighboring Chianti, was the first internationally recognized
winemaker to buy land here to make his now legendary super-
Tuscan Ornellaia. Based on a traditional Bordeaux blend, Ornellaia is bold, beautiful, and unabashedly nontraditional. It was
a big hit, and other winemakers soon followed in the hopes of
also making superpriced wines from these heretofore overlooked
plots.

In the shadows of this formidable new generation of international wines, local producers with older vineyards hidden in the
hills still struggle for recognition. Morellino di Scansano is the
best known of the Maremma's traditional wines. At its best, this
Sangiovese-based blend can approach the sublimity of Brunello
di Montalcino made just over the inland side of the same mountain, Monte Amiata. Sometimes, as with many Sangiovese-based
wines, Morellino can be aggressively tannic, especially when
young, and therefore not the easiest sell to an American looking
for a bottle to drink tonight.

Overlooking terraced vineyards and the azure Tyrrhenian Sea
in the distance, the tasting was held at a long table, with a dozen
glasses at each setting. At the lunch were eight winemakers ranging from the fastidious Adolfo Parentini of Moris Farms to the

ACQUA COTTA

SERVES 6

This is a classic recipe from the Maremma. Acqua Cotta (literally "cooked water") is a traditional dish originally made by the area's farmers. With few ingredients and needing little time, Acqua Cotta manages the alchemy that comes from great recipes: it transports you to its place of origin while also being delicious. Acqua Cotta also welcomes improvisation. If I have a few leaves of sage, for example, I'll throw them in as well. Once, when I made this for my father, I added some cooked fagioli (kidney beans).

4 TABLESPOONS OF A STRONGLY AROMATIC OLIVE OIL (FROM THE MAREMMA OR PUGLIA, IF POSSIBLE)

3 LARGE ONIONS, CHOPPED

2 TOMATOES, CHOPPED

A FEW LEAVES OF FRESH BASIL, TORN

1 STALK CELERY, CHOPPED

6 CUPS OF CHICKEN BROTH

¼ POUND GRATED PECORINO CHEESE

1 LOAF CRUSTY BREAD, SLICED 2 TO 3 INCHES IN DIAMETER AND ¼-INCH THICK

3 QUARTS WATER

6 LARGE EGGS

Pour the olive oil into a large saucepan. Add the onions. Cook on medium heat until clear, 3 to 5 minutes. Add the tomatoes and continue to cook with the basil and celery. Once soft, about 10 minutes, add the broth and simmer for 15 minutes.

(recipe continues)

Meanwhile, sprinkle grated Pecorino on small slices of crusty bread and toast on a ridged cast iron skillet or under a broiler.

Bring the water to boil in a five-quart pot. Poach the six eggs (or one per person) for 1 to 2 minutes, or as long as it takes for them to clarify. Make sure to leave enough space between the eggs so that they do not overlap. In each bowl, lay a few pieces of toast, ladle on one egg, and then add some broth. *Buon appetito!*

---

easygoing Gianpaolo Paglia of Poggio Argentiera. Some of the vineyards sought to improve the traditional Morellino; others had planted new varietals with a clean slate. All were there to get us to buy wine.

Becky and I were embarrassed by all the attention. Our neighborhood store had been open only one year. We took assiduous notes and tried to remain poker-faced to avoid showing favoritism while clinking glasses and trying to keep up with the heaping plates of pappardelle (wide pasta noodles favored in the area) and cinghiale (wild boar).

We struck up a conversation with Roland Krebser, a quiet Swiss transplant and winemaker for a German-owned vineyard in the heart of the Maremma. Over the course of the lunch, Becky and I bonded with the genial organic farmer so focused on making the best possible product. Then we left.

On the heels of such a memorable experience, we decided to take up Fabio Burlotto on his offer to visit his family's estate in Piedmont.

After six hours on the autostrada with my wife, mother-in-law, cousin, and son squeezed into our convertible with a broken top, we knew we weren't in Tuscany anymore. Gone were the silhouettes of cypresses bathed in a golden glow. Gone was the lapping Mediterranean. Gone also was the sun. We were shivering.

But we were finally in Verduno, at the front gate to G.B. Burlotto, one of Barolo's oldest-school producers. Looming behind the cast iron entrance was a meticulously painted façade emblazoned with "Comm. G.B. Burlotto" on a scroll. Underneath were depictions of three coats of arms and twenty-three medals.

It was also one of the few times I've visited Piedmont as an adult, and it made me realize how poorly I remembered Italy's most famous wine area. In addition to being colder, this northern region was more sparsely populated than I recalled. Burlotto's headquarters, an assembly of stunning old buildings in the center of town, was practically the only thing going on there. We were just an hour away from Turin, and there were more tractors than cars. For someone used to the scrum at the beaches of Versilia, packed with vacationing Florentines and Milanese, discovering Verduno was like finding rural Iowa next to Detroit.

I'd always been led to believe that in Italy the farther north one goes, the more developed, the more innovative, the more hell-bent on progress it becomes. Burlotto's fattoria in Verduno, I imagined, would be like the Ferrari factory in Maranello, a famous icon that is now completely enveloped in urban sprawl. In reality, vineyards surround Verduno, and they have for centuries. On steep hills where tractors can't climb, vineyard workers tend the vines. By the roadside are haylofts and dung piles. Burlotto isn't biodynamic or officially organic (another laborious certification in Italy), but it's definitely green. Like many well-regarded vintners, their carbon footprint has always been small. That's just how they make wine.

Fabio was also more at ease than I'd remembered. Gone was the wall-eyed aristocrat in the Hermès sneakers I'd met in New York the previous year when he came to our store on a sales call. Then again, I'm not sure how comfortable I would have been being dragged around from retailer to retailer by a sales rep eager to show off his trophy vintner. In place of the reluctant marketer was a soft-spoken, more confident winemaker wearing New Balance this time and in his element.

He was eager to show us around, and we were happy to be warming up. Our first stop was the cellar. Burlotto's stone vaults, wine-stained floors, and ancient barrels offered a wine cellar as you always imagined it, a far cry from the stainless-steel vats and vaguely nuclear aesthetic that characterize many contemporary cellars. The competition may replace small Slovenian oak barrels (called *barriques*) every year to beef up the flavor, but here they still reuse massive old casks that impart a more mellow richness by limiting the wine's contact with wood. One was even emblazoned with the seal of former King Vittorio Emanuele. And for good reason: Burlotto was a supplier to the royal household when Italy still had kings. The king brought Burlotto Barolo to fortify himself on an 1899 expedition to the North Pole, so convinced was he of its value. I could just imagine the packing list: Sleds? Check. Sled dogs? Check. Barolo? Check.

At every turn was a reminder of that illustrious history: pictures of his grandfather, great-grandfathers, and great-great-grandfathers. As we made our way through a series of interconnected structures passing through various courtyards and under loggias (open walkways facing gardens), we finally came to the "tasting room." Actually, that is a misnomer: this wasn't a rec room slapped together to shill plonk to busloads of tourists out of plastic cups; this was a seventeenth-century chapel with magnificently restored frescoes and shafts of light dramatically streaming down from the cupola. After Fabio left to retrieve the wines, Becky and I looked at each other and let out a collective "Can you believe this?"

Burlotto, it became immediately clear, is a marketer's dream: an authentic brand with a distinguished heritage, a product of passion rather than venture capital. The vineyard reminded me of Florence's now-famous Farmacia di Santa Maria Novella, a drugstore that has been in business since 1381, whose lily-infused soaps are available at Barney's.

When Fabio returned, he laid out a line of dusty bottles. Our first taste was of Pelaverga, that local and lesser-known varietal we had first tasted when Fabio visited our store. In New York, the wine had struck us as delicate and mysterious. Here, it was Piedmont translated into liquid. Talk about terroir! Our first Nebbiolo, the grape from which Barolo is made, was from their Monvigliero vineyard, a mile away from Burlotto's Verduno winery.

Facing south, the vineyard produces riper grapes; the taste is slightly fruitier than typical Barolo but also a tad friendlier—still refined but something a California Cab drinker might enjoy. Slowly, we worked our way through the lineup until we reached the climax, Barolo Cannubi, named after the most famous vineyard in Italy. Cannubi is so well regarded that it's now actually split up among a number of the area's most legendary producers, such as Giacosa and Mascarello.

Ironically, as I've discovered in the store, Barolo is a harder sell than one would imagine for a wine of such world renown. As esteemed as the "king of wines" is, Barolo suffers from an image problem. Like Sangiovese, Nebbiolo can be tannic when young, particularly in off years when the weather is harsher than usual. Until the 1970s, traditional but unsophisticated winemaking often compounded the problem. Just as with old French Burgundies, also grown in colder climes, Barolo's good years were transcendent, but the bad were almost undrinkable: thin, alcoholic, and often bitter. The macho rep still lingers, and, not surprisingly, Barolo is still a steakhouse mainstay. But the reality is different, as we were about to find out. At last we were to taste the pinnacle of Italian winemaking from a banner year, meters from where it was pressed—still completely by human feet.

As Fabio poured the wine, one thing was immediately clear: Pale Nebbiolo is not a swaggering grape. Compared to Opus One, that paradigm of Napa inkiness made from Cabernet Sauvignon, this wine was almost translucent. Green tea to California's Aqua Velva, the delicate smell was more intriguing than in your face. As we sipped, we were slowly enveloped. The scent lingers but whispers. Was that truffle? Were those plums? Barolo, we were reminded, is a wine that beckons you to discover it rather than broadcasting itself from afar.

It was the perfect moment: the chapel and the angels, the elixir and the shafts of light descending from the heavens. I'm surprised I didn't end up speaking in tongues. I was shivering again.

"I'm hungry," my son, Luca, cried, jolting me out of my reverie. "Let's eat," I suggested.

Four hours later, we finally stumbled out of La Morra restaurant, testament to the selfless generosity and true gentlemanliness of a shy Italian vintner saddled with five American dinner companions. The meal was a haze. Truffles, I'm sure. Wild boar? Yes. That too. What really lingers is the magic of that low-key sophistication and of what was in that glass at the chapel.

Our shop has remained one of Fabio Burlotto's most ardent supporters.

During our second year, I also learned an invaluable shortcut: to find good wine, turn the bottle around. On the back of each bottle you will find who brought it into the country. The imprimatur of a good importer, I discovered, is often a reliable guarantee of quality. The talent scouts of wine, importers are the intrepid explorers hunting for the next barn find. The best of them, like Kermit Lynch, are legendary for their ability to uncover gifted winemakers. Lynch, who also operates a San Francisco wineshop thanks to more lenient Californian liquor laws, was one of the first entrepreneurs to bring over small production wines.

In New York, Neal Rosenthal is one of a handful of these importer-tastemakers (who include Joe Dressner, Peter Weygandt, and Michael Skurnik, though some contend that Skurnik has grown too big to be quite as much of a guarantee) whose names are synonymous with quality. Each one has his niche. Rosenthal is well known for a French-heavy selection of offbeat winemakers. His prices are a little higher than those of some of his competitors, but his wines are captivating. A Rosenthal wine is always a discovery.

In 2010, I finally visited Rosenthal at his home-cum-headquarters in Shekomeko, New York. After five years of doing business together, Neal had invited me to lunch. Saddled between two Dutchess County horse farms, his converted barn has been modernized with weathered steel and cherry cabinetry. The house is immaculate, like its owner. A sixty-four-year-old with a thirty-one-inch waist, Rosenthal is lean and focused and not at all the ebullient R. W. Apple of my mind's eye. Lunch consisted of three things: a bowl of artisan pasta, half a homegrown heirloom tomato, and two one-third glasses of 1996 Brovia Dolcetto.

The fastidiousness of its preparation was mesmerizing. I watched Neal carefully unwrap the artisan pasta and delicately plunge two fistfuls into the boiling water. He gingerly scooped three spoons per bowl of imported tomato confit into each bowl. I must have smiled when he cut the half tomato at the table, as I imagined Lisetta would have been hysterical watching such measured precision. I was also intrigued by his calculated choice of wine. Dolcetto often is considered a pleasant but throwaway wine from the Piedmont region, which is so revered for its Barolos. Neal, it was clear, wanted to let me know that he could surprise me with a judicious choice, a consciously nonblockbuster red that would be more impressive than a run-of-the-mill 95-point *Wine Spectator* selection. And it was. At the end of the meal, Neal opened up a cabinet filled with rows of beautifully packaged honeys that he also imports. He reached for a jar. He unscrewed the top. We sniffed: chestnut. "Almost too intense," he told me. He put the jar back into the cabinet. He reached for another: acacia. "Sunshine!" Then Alpine wildflower. "Floral, crisp." The aromas were complex, like wine bouquets. In all, we smelled eight honeys. Neal did not ladle out a single spoonful to taste.

Throughout lunch, conversation was cordial but restrained. Part of it, of course, had to do with the awkwardness of two strangers. Who was I but some small retail account in one of the six states in which he distributes? Aside from a brief diatribe on the importance of proper storage of wine from the vineyard until the wineshop, I couldn't tell you one thing Neal said. There weren't anecdotes presented to enchant. There was just Neal Rosenthal, the long-distance runner who is exacting, driven, and restless. I discovered that he was not destined to become my life-long friend, but I am glad he is looking out for the quality of the wines I buy from him.

Looking back, I wish more of my wine-related meals had been so restrained. During that second crush year, we often were invited for magnum-draining bacchanals that we had not yet learned to refuse. I was starting to groan from all that bonhomie. According to our records, Becky and I bought 479 bottles of wine from the store that year. Sure, we had guests at our place, but that is still a lot of alcohol. I was heavier then, too, 183 pounds on my slight five-foot-ten-inch frame. As the year ended, we were laden with debt. And although we weren't exactly going backward, we weren't going far enough ahead to make a real dent. We were bloated and anxious. I had imagined that renovating a building and caring for a little boy and starting a new venture and leaving a familiar livelihood would be challenging. I was, though, beginning to feel beaten down.

Life at Cannizzaro seemed to be mirroring our stress: Liset-ta's memory was faltering. She was losing interest in food (and not even making her famous salt). My father was tired too. Even Luca, our gentle son, was scraping through his terrible twos. As the year ended, sales were up, but spending—and strain—was up higher. My 3 a.m. mantra was "Will we make it?"

chapter 5

FERMENT

FERMENTATION, when grape juice turns alcoholic, is a critical phase of winemaking.

To natural vintners, an organically grown grape has everything it needs to turn itself into wine. The pulp is filled with natural sugars, and the skin is home to wild yeasts, which turn sugar into alcohol. Once the skin is broken, the sweet juice is exposed to the yeasts, and winemaking begins. Fermentation continues until all the sugar has been broken down into alcohol or the juice's alcohol level reaches around 15 percent, at which point the yeasts will die. Indigenous yeasts, the naturalists observe, give wines their individual character.

But there are pitfalls. Fermentation needs to happen at the right temperature for the yeasts to do their work. There may be undesirable bacteria, which can turn a harvested crop into vinegar. Without enough nutrients, the grape juice will give off foul-smelling hydrogen sulfide gas. And if grapes are not harvested at the peak of perfection, they may not have enough sugar to turn into alcohol.

With these perils, most producers kill existing yeasts by

adding sulfur dioxide (the stuff that gives people headaches) to the must, the sloshy grape juice. They toss in commercial yeast and nutrient packets to keep the fungi well fed and carefully control the temperatures. To salvage underripe crops, vintners may add sugar to boost the alcohol or use reverse osmosis, a process that removes water from the juice to enhance its concentration. To offset the bitterness of stems, seeds, and other detritus that can be crushed inadvertently along with the grapes, producers may sprinkle bacteria powder to jump-start malolactic fermentation for a smoother, more buttery finish. The result is wine that is consistent from vineyard to vineyard and from year to year.

These manipulations may sound very Dr. Strangelove, but many consumers want wine that tastes consistent from year to year. Does it seem so evil to consider that with so many potential pitfalls, you would not be proactive? Especially if it's only for one brief step. After all, if you can make it through this crucial phase, the rest should be pretty straightforward, right?

AFTER TWO YEARS IN BUSINESS, everyone told us we were home free. If we had survived the first twenty-four months, the period in which 90 percent of new ventures fail, we were told we'd be on easy street. Well, not quite. At the end of 2007, before the economy started tanking, our wineshop, which had been featured in so many magazines and named to so many top-ten lists, took a radical turn for the worse.

It started with Janet. Of course, Becky and I were still agonizing over our talented but troubled wine director. Janet was passionate and driven; she knew so much about wine, and she loved selling. "So she borrowed our car without permission?" we asked ourselves. So she wrote herself an expense reimbursement check without telling us? So she disappeared for two extra weeks in Burgundy after we had given her a plane ticket? Even making out with Armando at our holiday party could possibly be excused. But we saw a pattern we could no longer deny.

We were terrified of letting her go. Janet had so many rare qualities. How, Becky and I wondered, would we ever find someone to take her place? Despite having had the shop for two years, we still felt like wine world outsiders. "It's not like we're going to find her replacement at Whole Foods," Becky added.

But under the pressure of the impending holiday season, we could tell that Janet's heart was no longer in her work for us. She didn't bound into the store, bursting with excitement over an impending delivery of Côte Rôtie. She didn't regale us with stories of great wines she'd tasted the night before. She no longer made lists of potential fat cat customers. Instead, she withdrew.

The time had come, we realized, to part ways. When we sat her down, Janet seemed relieved. We were less so. Janet had been with us since the beginning, in mid-2005. She had known Luca since birth. Now she was leaving, and we were going to have to move forward on our own.

Becky organized a going away party. Because Christmas was approaching, we gave Janet some money to tide her over during the winter months. There were some heartfelt good-byes.

Then, with the holidays upon us, we had to get back to work. The end of the year is important to every retailer, but especially to wineshops, which can average 60 percent of the total year's gross in the five weeks between Thanksgiving and New Year's Eve.

Three weeks after Janet's send-off, one of my in-laws forwarded me an e-mail wine solicitation he had just received from the "Thoreau Wine Society." It was signed by Janet.

> *Chers Amis,*
>
> *As revenge for an internment by this complex lexicon I take particular joy in forcing my rampant Americana onto the French (5 daily hours of classroom French, I'm not sure anymore what language I'm writing). Over the Hospices de Beaune weekend, our Rhodanian house-guests were tortured by my Cole Porter songs and they tortured back with their militant answer to pinot Noir—syrah, the more reliable, more tenable of the cepages, the best coming from the Andes-like cliffs that hang over the Rhône river in the climactic Côte Rotie. . . .*

Over the next few days, former design clients, college chums, and regular customers started asking me about Janet's new venture. Was I involved? Could it actually be the same Janet Hoover? Yes, it was. That was the familiar writing I had edited while she was on our staff.

Janet, it turns out, had cleared out more than our cache of Savennières, a Loire Valley white prized among oenophiles, when she left. She had lifted our mailing list! And now she was selling wine to my customers. I guessed that she hadn't realized the significance of what she had done. I sent her an e-mail explaining that a mailing list was property and that using it amounted to theft. The next week, she sent out another solicitation. I tried to put it out of my head. Two weeks later, Janet did it again. I told her that in addition to breaking our employment agreement, she was selling alcohol without a license and could get into big trouble. But her newsletters kept coming.

Becky and I were stunned. With our long history and her well-managed exit, we wondered what would compel Janet to ignore us. To sue her seemed like overkill. We just wanted her to stop. But how?

Then I made my first big mistake. I called the State Liquor Authority in the hopes that she would listen to them. I imagined that they would give her a stern warning about breaking a rule, and that would be it. But after reviewing her e-mails, the intake officer told me that this case was out of his jurisdiction, as she did not have a liquor license. The authority, he explained, could take enforcement procedures only against licensees!

Meanwhile, our business was swamped. Our fifteen-year-old Volvo station wagon was not cutting it. Even with 178,800 miles, the car was indestructible, but the logistics were unreal. To make a delivery to *Condé Nast*, for example, we had to go through two layers of security in the building's basement before being allowed to drop off a package, a forty-minute ordeal if we were lucky enough to find a spot in the loading dock next to Times Square. Otherwise, one person (usually me) circled while the other, usually Suzanne, ducked in with the delivery. In 2006, one law firm ordered 175 bottles of champagne to be delivered to ninety-seven different locations. Multiply each gift by forty minutes and you can start to imagine what we were up against. In the end, we had to messenger hundreds of bottles individually, sucking up the $9 delivery cost. Like most other wineshops, we typically mark up only 15 percent on a bottle of champagne, so we were losing $1.50 on each bottle we schlepped around town.

Strewn with Styrofoam shipping containers, piles of ribbon,

and huge bags of foam peanuts, the enoteca was fast becoming a dysfunctional Santa's workshop. On one side, John, our stalwart wine salesman, was busy tying hundreds of ribbons. I sat behind six-inch stacks of UPS labels. Becky came in after work to organize and inspect every shipment before it was sent. And every other night there was an event run by Suzanne for which it all had to be put away. It was chaotic but exciting, like being among the runners on the floor of the stock exchange. At the end of each day, Becky and I dragged ourselves upstairs to our apartment, exhausted but still high from the bustle. We were enervated. No, we were stoked. And invariably, Luca, his baby-sitter, and our dog, Guendi, were nuzzled against each other and sound asleep.

On New Year's Day 2008, it all came, as it does every year, to a screeching halt. However, unlike the partiers in their funny hats, our hangover lasts through February. It's as if after all that holiday revelry, no one can bear to see another bottle of alcohol for two months. For most stores, midwinter is a time to recoup and take stock. In bigger shops, clerks often loiter on the floor. In our shop, it was Guendi, who now lounged by my feet on the enoteca's stone floor. It's a comedown from the Christmas frenzy but a welcome one. For some.

Janet's e-mails kept coming. More customers were confused. "Are these yours?" they asked. Worse, some couldn't wait to tell me that they had just placed orders with "us" via e-mail. Then the tax bill came. It turned out Janet had neglected to file three quarterly sales tax returns from a year and a half ago. The government wanted its money. So did everyone else. No amount of Becky's reassurance ("That's when Luca was born; of course you were distracted." "And don't you remember that we were renovating the upstairs apartments too?") could assuage my self-loathing. How could I have not followed up on something so basic? Why did I not check up after a twenty-nine-year-old? I messed up. Oh, boy.

Several weeks later and after many nights spent upright from three to four o'clock, I went downstairs to open the store and found water cascading from every crack. The bottles were getting soaked. Our plumber deduced that we had a burst pipe behind a second floor bathroom. Within minutes, the pipe was patched. Total disaster was narrowly avoided, but I was more on edge than ever.

A few friends were starting to admit doubts about my life-changing experiment. An English chum who prides himself on his brutal honesty told me, "Close the store. Sell the building." "You've already maximized your return," the buyer of distressed media properties advised. "Move on," he insisted. I countered, stuttering things like "But the market is still going up."

What I really wanted to say to everyone was, "But what about that Pinot Noir we discovered on the second floor? How about those smiling faces in the store? And our home on top of it all? What about doing what you love, living where you work, creating the life you dreamed of? Thomas Jefferson was broke when he died. Would you have told him to sell Monticello?"

Underneath all that cynicism, I wanted to tell my pal with the shimmering shoulder-length hair, "You're a romantic. And what you really think is that I'm too attached—to the store, to the building, to the way of life—and you're afraid I could get hurt."

BEFORE THE RENOVATION, the store had been featured on *Law & Order* as two prostitutes duked it out on the sidewalk in front of our graffiti-covered roll-down gates. *Law & Order* always seemed to shoot in our neighborhood when they had to fish a floater out of the East River, so I was not immediately alarmed when a guy with a badge hung around his neck strolled in. "Extra," I thought. Then he asked for me and started snapping pictures as if he were documenting a crime scene. Suddenly, I was no longer watching a police drama, I was starring in one.

John Watts, who bears more than a passing resemblance to Barney Fife, told me that I had done a bad thing. Actually, many bad things. In our back room, we had, he said after he paused, "events." There was no use denying it because they had already confirmed it. "Agents requested information," and, he nodded knowingly, "you sent it."

"But of course you can have tastings in the enoteca," I responded. "It's right on our website."

"You did not have tastings," he countered. "You had *events*. Tastings are educational."

"But we typically pour six different wines while our sommelier explains their origins and guides our guests through tasting each example. How's that not educational?"

"You had food."

"Yes," I said. "We often pair wines with antipasti from Barbarini, the Italian restaurant around the corner."

Mr. Watts was losing his patience: "The law says you can serve tidbits. And you had food."

I was starting to feel like Kafka's Josef K. I knew food was a critical issue for the authority. In New York State (although the laws vary from state to state), there are two basic categories of license: "on-premise," which allows consumption of alcohol on the spot, such as restaurants and bars, and "off-premise," which authorizes retailers to sell sealed wine and liquor bottles to be drunk somewhere else. However, the law also allows for wineshops to conduct tastings and to offer tidbits to accompany the wines. I just assumed that tidbits meant "little things to eat."

John and I went back and forth. I started to get strident. I asked him if this meant that the three dozen wineshop events on LocalWineEvents.com that week were also illegal, since the site mentioned dinners with winemakers and other tidbit-heavy stuff that, frankly, seemed pretty appealing to people interested in wine.

Special Agent Watts turned stony and went back to documenting our glass racks and cocktail napkins. Once he determined that we did not have a kitchen, a big no-no for a retail store, he seemed to soften. "You should ask your lawyer," Watts suggested. "He'll know the difference." And then, like all the detectives you see on *Law & Order,* he said, "You'll be hearing from us."

The next day I did not contact the lawyer who had helped us with our permit. I went to see one of the city's foremost liquor law attorneys. I spoke to the counsel to Acker Merrall & Condit, the country's oldest wine merchant, as well as to the restaurateur Brian McNally, a former commissioner for the State Liquor Authority. From around the Formica-covered conference table, the old pro ambiguated: "The law is fuzzy. You should ask one of your wine distributors. They know the ins and outs." Then he blurted, "Besides, I can't represent you anyway. One of my clients is Janet Hoover."

Oh, you mean the Janet Hoover who may have complained (or had someone protest on her behalf) to the New York State

Liquor Authority in response to my complaint?! Somehow—though I had no proof, I could only imagine her showing up at the State Liquor Authority's offices sporting her bright red glasses—the SLA took more issue with our tastings than with someone selling wine without a license.

When I asked Armando, he had a more informative take: the key is to remember that you are not charging for experiences, he advised, but for educational materials. From what he recommended, customers should really be charged $75 a head for leaflets with tasting notes. Technically, he pointed out, the wine and food are free.

Despite this insight, Armando still could not define a tidbit. I sifted through the entire New York Alcoholic Beverage Control code from the State Liquor Authority and also could not find a definition. Then I found an article from the *New York Times* that explained how fudgeable it all seemed. Florence Fabricant described the wide range of foods that were served at tastings at some of the best-known liquor stores in Manhattan. For example, 67 Wines & Spirits, a large Upper West Side store that has been in business since 1941, even has a kitchen. Mario Batali's Italian Wine Merchants serves five-course wine dinners out of its shop. Chelsea Wine Merchant, as the article described, has a lower-level dining room that it uses for catered meals. What do these guys know that I don't?

Until I figured out exactly what was permissible, I suspended all enoteca activity. Since the tastings were much more profitable than meager midwinter wine sales it hurt. But we had no choice. After a year and a half, Suzanne left to become a sommelier, a logical step for her but a painful one for us. To make matters worse, we were behind on our mortgage again.

I decided to take a radical step to shore up our finances. I sold our well-known store fixture, the one featured in all the articles, my 1967 Ferrari 330 GT 2+2.

"Boo hoo," you must be thinking, "Poor schnook had to get rid of his fancy car." You're right.

Then again, the Ferrari was more than just a car or a store fixture. As mythic as a 2001 Quintarelli Barolo or a 1997 Sassicaia, this 1960s gentleman's Gran Turismo was the embodiment of that dolce vita dream life that opening a wineshop was supposed to offer. Although meant for streaking across Europe in style, even when sitting behind the wheel in the middle of the store, it was hard not to feel like Marcello Mastroianni. The car embodied style, freedom, and ease with a Continental flair. It was also damn beautiful. I loved its evanescent silver blue paint color and Borrani wire wheels and listening to the thrum of those twelve cylinders.

Some attributes that I admired about the car were similar to what drew me to wine: I loved the smell of leather and wood and gasoline—all adjectives used to describe wine. (Good Rieslings famously often have a "petrol" nose.) I loved the nuance: the machined ashtray inlaid with crossed enamel flags and the pistol grip shift lever.

I was, however, a little less crazy about actually driving it. The racing-derived clutch was too heavy. The enormous wooden steering wheel could have been used to steer a yacht. It took twenty minutes to warm up. None of that really mattered because before I had the store, the Ferrari spent much of its time at the mechanic, another connection to Italy albeit via the White Plains, New York, garage.

A specialist in vintage Italian autos, Domenick's European Car Repair "maintained" the Ferrari. In truth, in the ten years I owned the car, the shop never quite finished the work. But that was okay, because Domenick's was equally casual about the bills. During those years, I also became very fond of the shop's owners, Domenick Spadaro in beret and zip-up blue suit and his sons, Santo and Frank. One of the benefits of owning the car was that I got to eat biscotti and discuss mysterious rumbles and electrical quirks with the Spadaro family.

I got a nice offer from a Swiss collector, who dispatched his mechanic to inspect the car. His *jah* of approval was quickly followed by a wire transfer. I flung open the store's double doors and drove her out onto the sidewalk, where the shipper quickly loaded her into a large transport truck.

During that dark year in the middle of the recession, I also learned that I could be happy and miserable at the same time, especially in Italy during the summer.

Becky and I had a dazzling lunch at Lorenzo, the two-star Michelin restaurant in Forte dei Marmi owned by Lorenzo Viani, a passionate fisherman turned equally fanatical restaurateur. Lorenzo's fans include Giorgio Armani and Sirio Maccioni, owner of the famed New York restaurant Le Cirque, which is reputed to have been inspired by Lorenzo's place. Lorenzo's trademark is impeccably prepared, swimming-that-morning seafood.

We started with a local favorite, red mullet fillets (the firm fish tastes clean and fresh with a brininess that was prized by the

BAVETTE SUL PESCE
DA LORENZO
("LORENZO'S FISH LINGUINI")

SERVES 4

In this signature pasta dish from one of Italy's foremost seafood chefs, bavette, curved linguini, is cooked like risotto, but the preparation is quick and easy. The only trick is to use the freshest fish.

4 TABLESPOONS EXTRA-VIRGIN OLIVE OIL

I GARLIC CLOVE

I HOT PEPPER

6½ OUNCES CHOPPED MIXED SQUID, CUTTLEFISH, AND CRAYFISH, CLEANED

⅓ CUP DRY WHITE WINE

10 OUNCES BAVETTE PASTA (LINGUINI MAY BE SUBSTITUTED, ALTHOUGH IT LACKS BAVETTE'S SAUCE-CUPPING CONVEX CURVES)

2 CUPS WARM WATER

PARSLEY (TO GARNISH)

SALT

Sauté the oil, garlic, and pepper in a medium-hot large cast iron pan. Add the seafood. Bathe everything in the white wine and reduce the heat to low. Cook for a few minutes until the seafood has lost its translucency. Then add the bavette to the mixture, adding the warm water and constantly stirring with a wooden spoon until the bavette is al dente (8 to 10 minutes). Salt to taste.

Romans, who kept them as pets) baked with marinated vegetables flavored with celery; an octopus salad with potatoes, green beans, and Jerusalem artichoke purée; and a heaping platter of melt-in-your-mouth-tender tiny roasted squid.

Then came the pastas: ravioli stuffed with sea bass in a squid and crab sauce (ravioli ripieni di branzino in salsa di totani di sabbia e granchio), risotto with zucchini flowers, gratinéed red crawfish flavored with marjoram, and a sublime, disarmingly simple bavette (a curvy linguini) with a seafood sauce.

We were already undoing our pants' buttons when the main course arrived. Lorenzo brought out one of his favorite dishes: slow-cooked salt cod over chickpeas, pickled onions, and tomatoes. My father dived into a "tricolor" lobster salad with garlic, basil, and apple vinegar dressing. Luca gobbled up the Saint Peter's fish (another prized Mediterranean species with a delicate and flaky texture) bathed in a clam and crustacean sauce.

To add to the pleasure, Chiara, Lorenzo's daughter and my friend, had brought over a bottle of Radikon from her equally amazing wineshop around the corner from her father's famed eatery. Although not particularly well known in the United States, Radikon is one of the originators of Italy's natural wine movement. The Friulian producer makes rich whites with an almost sherrylike nuttiness. They are wines to be savored. We luxuriated.

Because I am his daughter's pal, Lorenzo tore himself away from charming a table of Russian oligarchs (the bread and butter of this resort town, Forte dei Marmi) to teach me, the rookie wineshop owner, how to "taste" by smearing my hands with Domaine de la Romanée Conti—one of the most expensive wines in the world—and then pressing my nose into my wine-soaked palms. Chiara stood by with one of those forced "there-goes-

Dad-again" smiles. Then Lorenzo launched into a romantic fish story that involved tanned *bagnini* (lifeguards) pulling in nets at dawn. My father and Lisetta, familiar with the tales, decided to start home without us.

On the drive back home, Becky and I described our favorite dishes. I was still gaga over the wine experience. She rhapsodized over the delicate fish pasta. "Now, that's something I'd like you to know how to make at home!" she exclaimed.

As we entered Cannizzaro, the phone was ringing; it was a physician at the Versilia hospital. "You should come now," he advised, and then hung up.

We saw my father and Lisetta lying side by side on gurneys. They were holding hands.

My dad had fallen asleep while driving on the way home and had plowed into a car dealership. The car was totaled, and he never drove again. Thank God, they were okay.

Within another month, in July 2008, we returned to New York to say good-bye to Guendalina, our wire-haired dachshund and my parents' wedding gift to us. At five, our beloved pet and symbol of our union developed pancreatic cancer.

Not long after the summer of 2008, I started to notice that Becky and I were drinking too much. For a long time, I think we rationalized it. We were having wine with dinner, just as we did in Italy. We willfully ignored the fact that the country wine we sip by the Tyrrhenian Sea is lower in alcohol (8 percent) than the higher-brow selections typically sold at our store (14 percent). Only Amarone, the beefy Venetian red made with dried grapes, neared 14 *gradi* (percent) when I was growing up. "Too heavy," Lisetta used to say whenever my father opened one of these "holiday" wines.

Our consumption was inching upward. What had started as a bottle split between the two of us had crept up to one and half and then two (a white for the starter and a red for the main course) and then culminated at two entire bottles of wine, plus digestivi.

When friends were over, our drinking spiked further. We'd enjoy a glass or two while cooking, have another couple with hors d'oeuvres, and then taste several different bottles with our guests.

What began as a civilized way to enjoy food and wine somehow had morphed into a daily stomach-swelling bacchanal. Becky and I were falling into bed, barely having brushed our teeth. I was sleeping fitfully. Too often, we awoke to empty bottles overflowing our recycling bin—and to my growing double chin.

"This is my job," I told myself. "Just my way of dealing with the stress." In addition to my parents' deteriorating health, the renovation was dragging and we were just barely keeping up with the mortgage. Worse, the store was posted frequently on the dreaded SLA blacklist, a shame roster of retailers who have taken more than thirty days to pay a bill. Reflecting both Prohibition morality and distributors' self-protection, state law requires that all alcohol purchases must be paid for within one month of delivery. Go a day over on a single bill and the wholesaler is obligated to report you to the state authorities. This is more crippling than shameful: listed retailers must pay cash on delivery for all subsequent shipments from *every* wholesaler until they are caught up. For an undercapitalized and semiorganized store like ours, the results were almost fatal. We had to continue to pay bills as we wrote out checks for more inventory, doubling our cash crunch.

I discovered that spending all that money was easier upstairs against the backdrop of the Brooklyn Bridge, one of my origi-

nal inspirations for buying the building and another beautiful
folly that turned out okay in the end. On one check-heavy day, I
parked myself on the sofa a few feet from Luca, who was happily
drawing with a crayon. I smiled thinking about father and son
working side by side and went back to my computer spreadsheet.
A few minutes later, I looked up. To my horror, Luca had continued his scribbling over the wood columns next to the sheet of
paper. The yellow scratchings over the newly sandblasted wood
looked like they could have been done by a drunk Cy Twombly.

"Luca," I yelled, "how could you?"

My son turned to me and deadpanned: "I'm sorry, Marco, but
I'm just two. You should be watching me."

"You're right," I admitted to the wise old man masquerading
as my toddler. If only you were old enough to work in a wineshop.

My brother Nicky told me not to worry. "At least you're not in
suburban Washington [where he lives]. For us, this recession is a
friggin' disaster. But New York," he said confidently, "will never
get hit hard."

No wonder I was hitting the sauce.

Unfortunately, I wasn't the only one having a hard time.

The New York wine world was also in tumult. Southern had
bought Paramount Brands in the previous year and then dis-
solved it. Armando was out of a job. Lovable Matt moved back
home. And Janet, we heard, discovered more than Pinot Noir in
Burgundy. She met a man and decided to stay. Despite the move,
her e-mails kept coming.

As the recession deepened, the sales reps' desperation reflect-
ed a larger tanking of the overall business. Some, it became apparent, were hurting even more than we were. Not surprisingly,
restaurants and high-end merchants were the most affected.

The winemakers were getting frustrated too. As disaffection spread, they started jumping from distributor to distributor in a veritable *Jersey Shore* of bed-hopping. Even to those in the trade, the changes were a blur. Adding to the uncertainty about sales, we often weren't sure from whom to buy what.

Southern found that doing business in New York was more difficult than in its native Florida. There were lots of parking tickets and union truckers with $120,000 salaries. According to Matt, Southern had underestimated the "appeal of the underdog." New York wine buyers liked "scrappy guys with small portfolios selling stuff that you could find nowhere else." New York wineshop owners pride themselves, Matt explained, on being inside and ahead of the curve. Despite its extraordinary portfolio of some of the world's most sought-after wines (like Burgundy's Morey, the Rhone's Beaucastel, and Alsace's Domaine Weinbach), Southern was snubbed by wine buyers who associated it with Yellow Tail, the immensely popular Australian wine that tastes like grape juice mixed with wood shavings. "Crass and commercial," store owners snipe as they grudgingly phone in more ten-case drops of Absolut vodka and Patrón tequila. In New York, Southern had nowhere near the 50 percent of floor space it typically commanded in other markets. With more than three hundred distributors, New York City has a lot more small guys with interesting wines than a state like California, which has only six distributors.

That same year, 2008, Robin Goldstein revealed on his blog, *Blind Taste,* that *Wine Spectator,* the most widely circulated and influential wine magazine, had given an "Award of Excellence" to a nonexistent restaurant in Milan. Osteria L'Intrepido was actually the creation of Goldstein, who submitted a fictitious application to be considered for the prize.

There was a huge outcry: "Hypocrites!" "What a farce!" said posters on the online bulletin boards. "The art of winemaking can do better without Corporate America's money-grubbing influence." There were confessions. On the *Dr. Vino* blog, one restaurant owner fessed up: "The award is meaningless but serves a purpose." "For a mere $250 a year, I get an award and my restaurant name listed on a nationally recognized website . . . press and recognition, all be it [sic] maybe only to the less informed but which make up probably a 80 percent share of my business. You find me another advertiser that does that for $250."

In retrospect, such fuzzy journalistic practices should not have been so surprising. Five years earlier, Amanda Hesser had reported in the *New York Times* that the *Spectator* had received 3,573 applications for Awards of Excellence and had doled out 3,360 commendations (for a 94 percent rate of excellence). All a restaurant had to do was submit a wine list, a sample menu, and a brief description of its wine program along with a $175 check. Except for eighty-nine winners of the magazine's top honor, the Grand Award, all were lauded sight unseen. As of 2008, the *Times* also reported that the fee had gone up to $250 and the glossy magazine granted four thousand awards, adding up to more than $1 million.

With its myriad 90-point wines and fat advertising revenue, America's premier wine magazine was not new to rumblings about its editorial independence. The discovery of this apparent pay-to-play scheme confirmed what shop owners had long mumbled to themselves as they stuck rows of shelf talkers promoting yet another *Wine Spectator*–blessed wine. In the *Spectator* world, as in Garrison Keillor's fictitious Lake Wobegon, every wine seems above average. Some wineries, which may or may not have bought the adjacent full-page ad, were even better than that.

In my preshop life, I was an assiduous reader of the *Spectator* and an enthusiastic seeker of its "Best Buys." Call me naive. But the numbers gave me confidence. Only later did I start to understand the dramatically flawed, albeit well-intentioned 100-point rating scale.

Of the 100 points available, Robert Parker, the influential wine critic commonly credited with creating the system, uses only 50. Every wine no matter how bad gets 50 points. The rest are graded in minute, single-point increments. Tellingly, Parker explains his system as just like college: 90 to 100 is an A, 80 to 89 is a B, 70 to 79 is a C, and below 70 is a D or F, "depending on where you went to school." The British wine writer Jancis Robinson uses a 20-point scale, just as the English do in their schools.

Needless to say, scores also depend on who is doing the reviewing. Parker tends to prefer thick, rich, and ripe wines, a style that seems to be going out of favor. A 2008 comparative study of Bordeaux ratings conducted by the Center for Hospitality Research at Cornell seems to confirm that the *Wine Spectator* and Stephen Tanzer, whose *International Wine Cellar* is also a highly influential review, march in lockstep with Parker. Robinson is Franco-centric with a few colonies such as Australia, New Zealand, and South Africa thrown in. Claret, what we call Bordeaux, is their holy grail. And many wines seem to be judged with this worldview in mind.

To add to the confusion, the same wine can taste vastly differently as it ages. I remember tasting a 2004 Domaine Leflaive

Montrachet with the renowned Burgundy critic Clive Coates in our enoteca. In 2006, it was lean and tight in a mildly unpleasant way. The wine's most pronounced characteristic was its mouth-puckering acidity. But Coates was able to use those faults to imagine what the wine would taste like in a few more years. The strong acidity, he predicted, would mellow into a deeper riper wine that still retained a crisp minerality. When I retasted the wine in 2009, I realized that Coates had been right. That stingy Chardonnay had blossomed into a huge and enormously satisfying wine. And, of course, bottle variation and the taster's mood can also skew a wine's rating.

From my perspective, four letters may be more helpful than 50 disguised as 100. They get you in the ballpark (i.e., A—once in a lifetime, B—big celebration, C—nice everyday wine, D—kind of crummy); the rest is where you and your preferences come in. A four-tier system seems to work for movie and restaurant reviews; why should wine be judged any differently?

It's easy to understand why a wine drinker would be tempted to follow straightforward rankings after reading much wine writing. Critics tend to talk in a shorthand that's intended to communicate an experience by using a universal vocabulary. Ironically, the result can be a metalanguage almost inscrutable to the outsider: "Notes of Oriental saddle leather?" "Black fruit?"

At the major seasonal tastings where distributors gather all their producers in a room, one invariably hears a wine geek giggling as he describes a Sauvignon Blanc as smelling of "cat's piss," a coded compliment that's supposed to show how inside you are but really ends up sounding kind of lame. Or someone will exclaim (just loud enough to be heard across the aisle), "Dirty socks!" while sipping a woodsy and very pricey Burgundy. In this topsy-turvy world, occasionally a hipster will shout, "That's hot!" which ironically is an insult, as "hot" wines are said to have too much alcohol. Imagine several hundred tipsy Trekkies wandering around a *Star Trek* convention and you get the vibe. Initially, we tried to bring some of these metaphoric descriptions to life by offering tastings that paired wines with the things they were said to taste like. For instance, we put cherries next to a cabernet that was said to have cherry aromas; we paired plums with Syrahs; we even found some gooseberries for Sauvignon Blanc. But it always felt as if we were trying to describe the taste of grapes by using some other food. We asked ourselves: "Why can't grapes taste like grapes?"

Some of our most successful wines (based on sales and customer feedback) garner comments that avoid fancy descriptors altogether. Our best-selling Sancerre, by Vacheron, has always been described as "Catherine Deneuve if she were a wine." It's oblique, yet our clients seem to get what we mean: elegant, refined, timelessly chic, if perhaps a bit chilly and remote.

Things started to turn around in July when we found our new wine director, Ryan Ibsen. A former sommelier whose résumé included two years at the New York restaurant of a world-renowned chef, Ryan brought a trained nose and a welcome professionalism. I would like to say that we found Ryan by soliciting recommendations from celebrated sommeliers and venerated distributors and by word of mouth or that we contacted the nation's best wine programs and inquired about their most talented graduates. We did all that. But we found our ace new wine director on Craigslist. Nearly 225 résumés later (along with butcher, sommelier seems to have supplanted DJ as cool job du jour), Becky and I met Ryan. A lanky Northwesterner, he had spent the last seven years as a sommelier in some of the best-known restaurants in Seattle (and before that he'd toured with his band for seven years). And he was tired of nights ending at four in the morning followed by days starting a few hours later. He was sick of all those "Yes, sir's" and "Right away, ma'am's" taking back perfectly good wine when a large-bellied oaf barked, "This is crap!" Soms, he sighed, spend an awful lot of time putting together wine programs (their lists) only to have customers pick the most or least expensive bottles while ignoring the rest of the offerings. "I'd spend months finding the feather-light Nebbiolo from the Valle d'Aosta [in the Italian Alps] only to have everyone order Sancerre."

In New York, many sommeliers seem to have been night people in previous lives. Far from the chubby French guy with the silver cup dangling from his neck, the current generation of soms tends to be gaunt, pale, and tattooed. Proud of their high-low inclinations, they are night crawlers and aesthetes. They are hip and discriminating and not afraid to let you know it. I remember one visit to Luca D'Attoma, winemaker at Tuscany's famed Le Macchiole and now producer of his own wines, organized by Acid Inc. Selections, his New York distributor. This particular sommelier, the head of wine buying for David Chang's (of Momofuku fame) empire, drank seven beers and took two Xanax on the way over, glasses of every wine offered at lunch (eight by my count), beers in the afternoon, and then a few more Xanax and a couple more bottles of wine that night. Confident, charming, knowledgeable, Julian was also a complete mess.

Between the customer kowtowing and the hard-driving lifestyle, it's no surprise that many sommeliers burn out and move to other wine-related enterprises. Some end up dragging around wine-filled rolling luggage as salespeople for distributors. Some take time off by working the harvest for a famous producer. A few become winemakers. Others take refuge in the comparative sanity of a retail store. Ryan was ready for something normal.

Immediately, he put his mark on our selections, and there was some friction. In his efforts to make our assortment stand out, occasionally, I thought, Ryan prized interesting over serviceable. We had wines from Marcillac, an obscure appellation in southwestern France, but no Amarone, the famed Venetian red pressed from dried grapes, in a store named Pasanella. Geographically, his preferences were like that famous *New Yorker* cartoon "View of the World from Ninth Avenue" by Saul Steinberg, placing the city as the center of the earth separated by the Hudson River from a thin brown strip representing "Jersey," behind which are a few rocks representing the US mainland. Farther away lies a blue sliver ("Pacific Ocean"), and in the distance sit three tiny landmasses labeled China, Russia, and Japan. In Ryan's case, the center of the world was France. Austria, Germany, and Italy were close by. In the distance, northern California and the Northwest were highlighted. But the rest of the planet was a far-off mass called the "New World." I had always wanted the store to have a geographically varied selection of the world's best artisan producers. I was as proud of our New Zealand Sauvignon Blancs as I was of our Sicilian Frappati.

As Ryan soon discovered, a retail wine selection can be a trickier challenge than a restaurant list. Instead of pairing two dozen wines to a specific menu, a store must maintain several hundred selections to accommodate a wide variety of foods and preferences. In addition, customers tend to be more tightfisted about drinking at home than when they go out to dinner. In our case, this means that four out of five bottles we sell are under $15.

Those bottles typically cost us $10 each, but in a restaurant Ryan could make that back on the first glass pour. Sold by the glass, the same bread-and-butter, ten-buck bottle brought in $50 in revenue! That $40 profit could be plowed back into acquisitions of unusual bottles he could then afford to hold on to for months or in some cases years.

Retailers, he soon discovered, do not have that luxury. Ryan wanted the cool stuff, but we also needed the staples. With 80 percent of the monthly budget going toward the least expensive wines, Ryan's appetite often exceeded the available dough.

However, he managed to cobble together a fascinating assortment for people who wanted some discovery with their spaghetti. The wine trade started coming. Even the sommelier for Thomas Keller's Per Se restaurant became a regular. Our family life improved as Becky no longer had to work the occasional evening or weekend in addition to her full-time job at Martha Stewart.

I was less thrilled when, in the fall of 2008, just as Agent Watts had predicted, I heard from the State Liquor Authority. After six months of silence, I received a "Notice of Proceedings to Cancel or Revoke" that listed an upcoming hearing for the following week. The triple whammy of the new restrictions on tastings, Suzanne's departure, and the recession's arrival meant that our events business had shriveled up. We were about to lose our license for something we no longer did and had no money to show for.

Stew Burg was infuriatingly lackadaisical. After taking a few days to return my frantic calls, he told me to authorize a plea of no contest and offer to pay some money. By the end of the week, the State Liquor Authority agreed. I paid the fine. And poof, my inquest was history.

Good news kept coming. Several months into Ryan's tenure, Martha Stewart proposed to celebrate *Martha Stewart Living*'s major fall issue by having a party—I mean a *tasting*—in the store. To some degree, the location made sense as our upstairs apartment was featured in the magazine that month. But we still appreciated her loyalty—and tacit stamp of approval. We knew that if Martha didn't love the store, she never would have suggested the event. For Martha, quality always comes first.

In preparation, it was now Becky's turn to pop Xanax as she organized an elegant party for a boss whose billion-dollar company was born from her ability to produce elegant parties. A few days before the event, Martha did a drive-by to inspect the last-minute preparations. In anticipation of her arrival, we straightened all the displays, every bottle was turned so all the labels matched, the floor glistened, and the cabinet pulls sparkled. We even double-checked our stacks of labeled plastic bins in the storage area. Candles? Check. Cocktail napkins? Check. Glasses? Check. Martha scanned the room, nodded in approval, and then made a beeline for the gussied-up storage area, where she immediately came upon the one thing we had not Pledged to death: a spoon she held up as if dangling a particularly smelly beetle. "You're going to polish all this, right?"

Despite the silverware scare, the party was spectacular, well attended, and fun. Martha also surprised Becky by presenting her with a huge trove of vintage china in a pattern she knew Becky had starting collecting to use for store events. She also decided to shoot an episode of her television show in our enoteca. This time the spoons were shiny, and the segment went even better than the party. Ryan was informative and articulate. Becky was radiant and charming. And I, rigid and sweaty, looked a little like Albert Brooks in *Broadcast News*. It didn't matter. After all the hardships that year—the Janet drama, the SLA inquest, the sold car, the dead dog, the money woes, and the flood that wasn't—things were looking up. Or so I thought.

chapter 6

BOTTLE

THE PUNT, that familiar dimple at the bottom of a bottle, encapsulates almost everything that I love about—and I am occasionally frustrated by—wine. Ubiquitous yet mysterious, that seemingly innocuous dent stands at the collision of history and hearsay.

One theory is that the punt is merely a remnant from a time when bottles were hand blown. Others contend that the dimple makes the bottle more stable and less likely to topple. Or that the depression collects sediment, preventing gook from reaching the glass. Or that the cleft increases the bottle's strength, allowing it to hold the high pressure of sparkling wine and champagne. Or that the recess permits bottles to be stacked end to end. Or that the concavity enhances the wine's color by working like a lens. Or that the punt just provides a comfy place for the pourer's thumb.

Cynics contend that the punt just takes up space, thereby giving customers the mistaken impression that they're getting more than they are. Pragmatists assume that the dimple merely serves to hold bottles in place as they whip by on conveyor belts studded with pegs during the filling process.

According to Danish legend, the punt was part of a secret language servants used to signal their masters about the reliability of their guests. A thumb in the cleft meant the guest was a pain in the ass.

One thing's for sure: the punt remains a bump up at the bottom of the bottle. 🙣

"How would you like to open a store up in Connecticut?" a vaguely familiar voice asked on the other end of the line? The caller, Tom Seiler, who had shopped in the store the previous week, explained that he wanted to create a Pasanella & Son as part of a large historic restoration of downtown South Norwalk, Connecticut. Lying at the mouth of the Norwalk River, South Norwalk once had been a bustling harbor town with handsome brick factories lining the port. Like many industrial cities, it had fallen on hard times. What remained were the factories and an attractive, if empty, center city.

With its good architectural bones and proximity to Greenwich and Darien, Tom saw Norwalk as having excellent potential. Affluent residents of neighboring towns were flocking to a handful of hip restaurants in the burgeoning downtown. The appeal, Tom explained, was that South Norwalk offered a "taste of New York without the traffic." "What they really want," he concluded, "are bottles of nice wine to take home." Genial Tom was gung ho to start immediately. "What do you think?" he asked.

"Hmm . . . maybe," I temporized as I mouthed "Oh, my God!" to Becky.

Expansion had not been part of our original idea, but this opportunity sounded too good to pass up. Tom had the space and would put up all the money. He proposed a setup fee and royalty checks based on gross sales. In return, we would design, construct, supervise, staff, and set up the initial buys and whatever else it took to get the store going. They would get a fully operational business with a rising name. It sounded pretty straightforward.

Negotiations took forever. The real boss, it turned out, was Tom's Darien neighbor, a New York real estate broker named Jim Quinn. Except for the Range Rover, Jim reminded me of my buff but belligerent former fish tenant. Having worked in a real estate firm out of college, I knew the type: gregarious but tough and wily too.

As the economy plummeted, we inked the deal. The only thing missing was the initial check. After a few weeks, Jim called to explain that cash was tight and he was about to send a payment for a quarter of what the contract stipulated. I told him I understood that real estate was hurting. During the next six weeks, I threw myself into the work and designed the entire store, including all the fixtures.

No money came.

I found the perfect manager in neighboring New Haven.

No money came.

I even got Domenick's to promise to consign us a vintage Lancia to use as a store display.

Still no money.

Meanwhile, Jim transferred Tom to another of his projects, and Jim was becoming harder to pin down. The new wineshop was losing steam. Over the next six months, we had a series of meetings, and finally, Jim explained that he was out of cash.

Yet three months after Jim asked to halt our collaboration

because he could not pay his debt to us, he applied for a liquor license using the Pasanella name!

Then came another ill-timed call. I didn't know exactly what to think when Armando called to ask if we could meet. I could sense the anxiety in his voice.

"Sure, come on over," I told him.

Armando showed up without his wheelie bag.

"You know how I value our friendship," he began.

Uh oh.

"You also know that I have started a new distributorship," he continued.

Super uh oh.

"I want to hire Janet."

I did not fall off my chair or make a witty retort.

"What?" I stammered.

"Well, she's talented," he started.

"And crazy—and she *stole* our mailing list!" I helped him finish.

"I just wanted you to know."

"Don't worry," he added, "she won't be calling on you."

A few weeks later, I was forwarded another of Janet's highfalutin e-mail sales pitches. Evidently, the plum job Armando had offered her wasn't enough to keep her from shilling her own stuff on the side.

In place of Janet's histrionics was Ryan's West Coast cool, even if he sometimes sounded more like a sommelier than a wine salesman.

"Do you have any Beaujolais nouveau?" I overheard a young woman ask while I sat in the enoteca reviewing bills.

Because I knew Ryan considered Beaujolais nouveau overhyped, my ears perked up.

"No, I'm sorry," he responded. "We don't really do nouveau."
"It's more of a mass-production thing," he added.

"Well, I was looking for something . . . you know . . . nice,
but," she stammered, "like not too expensive."

"Try these Beaujolais crus," he suggested, ushering her over
to wines that cost almost twice as much and were considerably
drier.

"Balanced tannins," he explained, "excellent structure."

I heard her take a breath.

"Elegant, refined," he continued.

Another pause.

"Great expression of Gamay."

"Good with pizza?" she ventured.

"Perfect," Ryan assured her as I heard the bottle clink onto
the marble counter.

I assume the woman bought the wine because I heard the
cash register open, but I'm less sure about whether she liked the
fancy Beaujolais as much as Ryan did.

The worst thing about Ryan—other than his tendency to
squirrel away dog-eared paper stacks—was that he didn't (and
still doesn't) know how to stop working. Like Neal Rosenthal,
Ryan is a runner, and they share a similar marathon mentality.
Both men push through the pain. So far, I haven't been able to
convince Ryan that you can stop and rest every once in a while.

After four years, John, our genial wine collector cum counter-
man, was also still with us and remained unruffled even as the
rest of the world became more unhinged.

As the recession deepened, one of our customers, a twentysomething dancer who lived around the corner with her Wall
Street trader boyfriend, went from a weekly drop-by for a Pinot

Grigio to calling just before closing to beg John to drop off a bottle of white wine on his way home. Eventually, she took to phoning John every morning to ask if he could bring bottles by 10 a.m. One day, she came to the door wearing nothing but a T-shirt and a little white powder under her nose. He declined her invitation to "join the party." A few months later, the sparkling woman he nicknamed Poule Blanche (after her favorite wine) disappeared along with her boyfriend.

With the economic downturn moving into its second year, John and Ryan's equanimity was rare in the wine business. Desperation was in full swing.

"Hi, Ryan, this is [insert name here] from [same], and I have a special deal on [stuff we can't seem to sell]. It's 90 points Parker and just flying out of here, and I was wondering if . . ."

"This isn't Ryan."

"I'd like you to meet [take your pick], the world's greatest winemaker. Can we stop by?"

"Hey, Ryan. Scott here. Just wondering if I could taste you on some [poorly made wine I can't seem to get rid of]."

"Didn't I just see you last week?" I would overhear Ryan saying.

Ring.

"Is Ryan there?"

Ring-ring.

"Is Ryan there?"

One afternoon Ryan popped out to grab a cup of coffee, and I took six messages. Even Joe with the ThinkPad was calling with "big news on price breaks."

Just when the reps thought it was all over, a bump appeared at the bottom of our bottle: people started drinking again. In the depths of the recession, customers began treating themselves to an affordable luxury, something guaranteed to bring pleasure at $10 a pop: a bottle of wine to have with dinner.

Ryan was also getting his sea legs. Instead of telling customers what they should like, he started asking them what they were having for dinner. "Thai food? Oh, try this Riesling. Hint of sweet that'll offset the spice." "Pasta with pesto?" "Have just the thing: Pigato from Liguria. Crisp, refreshing." "I just love this producer," he would gush, and then slay them with some anecdote about the winemaker and his mom.

Customers soon came clutching recipes:

"Lemon risotto?" "Moscato Giallo."

"Smoked trout?" "Grüner Veltliner."

"Grilled duck breasts?" "Bourgeuil."

Ryan was dazzling. He was like one of those winning game show contestants who never gets stumped. Our customers were delighted.

At the same time, he became even more inventive with pairings. On one table he clustered wines that were good with "Grilled Peaches, Wiener Schnitzel, Linguini & Clams" and on another "Cioppino, Chicken Pot Pie, Bresaola & Melon."

Ryan also learned to pick his battles. I knew he had hit his stride when a balding captain of industry–type blew in asking for a "$100 Cali Cab" and Ryan didn't flinch as he handed over a 2005 Paul Hobbs, a well-known California Cabernet Sauvignon. Gone were the days when he would spend a half hour trying to persuade a customer to spend half as much on an equally good wine he'd never heard of.

Meanwhile, I took the opportunity to do some belt-tightening. I cut down on hedonistic wine dinners. I limited myself to the

Wednesday tastings with sales reps. If I hadn't quite conquered the bills, I started to reign in my lifestyle.

For exercise, I began riding my old track bike again (I had been a bicycle racer in my youth). A bike enthusiast had even snapped a picture of me riding in Manhattan on my freshly painted turquoise fixie and posted "Awesome bike!" on his blog. Too bad someone added below: "Yeah, can you believe that's ex-pro [not true] Marco Pasanella? Dude looks like he should be driving a Volvo!" Little did he know. At least it was a start.

We were also determined to do what we could to boost neighborhood spirits as well as our own. Given that both Ryan and John had strong musical backgrounds (Ryan toured for seven years, and John played with the Steve Miller Band), I conscripted them into forming a store band. The Lees, as in the dead yeast at the bottom of the barrel that nevertheless sometimes can be used to richen wines like Muscadet, were born. Ryan was on keyboards and lead vocals, with John on guitar and yours truly on the tambourine. We were a motley crew. Our neighborhood jam sessions were populated by a ragtag band of players. There was an ancient drummer who always seemed to be half a beat behind, a would-be hippie couple who just wanted to sing songs of protest, and a few intrepid fans who were happy to sip wine in the back of the store. We never got that big recording contract, nor did we jam together more than a handful of times, but the Lees made our neighbors smile.

It was our turn to beam when the detectives returned. "I am an acquired taste," cracked one of them. Luckily, this time, they were famous actors instead of Agent Watts. In 2009, the television show *Law & Order: Criminal Intent* decided to shoot a scene in the store. "We want classy," the location scout explained. "Your place has it up the wazoo." Instead of ferreting out retailers going heavy on the tidbits, the TV cops, played by Vincent D'Onofrio and Kathryn Erbe, sought information about the suspect, a wine collector turned murderer. Okay, it wasn't exactly upbeat, but who was quibbling? It was national television, and they had agreed to allow one of our employees to be an extra. She was thrilled.

Becky still elbows me awake every time she stumbles upon the episode on late night TV.

We were still far from out of the woods, but I was more concerned with a threat that might cast a darker shadow over our business than the economic downturn: Governor Paterson was considering the sale of wine in grocery stores. In New York State, licensed liquor stores can sell wine and hard alcohol and supermarkets can sell only beer. Large grocery chains such as Whole Foods and Wegmans had been lobbying the governor to change the laws, and the governor was keen on getting his hands on the anticipated tax revenue increase.

I sent an editorial to the *New York Times*. Having written for the paper of record, I was fairly sure that I would never hear from them. Just because you've covered faucets for the "Home" section, that does not ensure that you will be taken seriously as an op-ed contributor. But I tried.

Common wisdom was that allowing wine to be sold in grocery stores would kill the little guys, like me. It would certainly make it more difficult for a small wineshop like mine but could be devastating for stores in rural areas. That's not why I wrote to the *Times*, though. I believe in open competition, even intimidating competition. It just has to be fair. I saw the proposed changes as a huge opportunity to serve our customers better while redressing outdated, irrational, and inequitable laws.

New York's Alcoholic Beverage Control code, which has governed the sale of wine, beer, and liquor since Prohibition was repealed in 1933, sometimes seems like a charmingly genteel relic of a bygone era, when buying wine for Sunday supper was regarded as the Devil's work. We still can't open before noon on Sundays.

Under the current law, our store can sell only wine and wine-related accessories, which include such timely and irresistible items as "audio cassette tapes, designed to help educate consumers in their knowledge and appreciation of wine."

If the big grocers were going to sell Côtes du Rhône, why, I reasoned, couldn't I sell baguettes and brie? Or artisan beer? Or reusable shopping bags (one Rochester store was recently fined $10,000 for doing that).

Why limit me to one store? How about letting me operate multiple locations just like the big-box retailers?

And while I was hardly going to stake my business on the Sunday brunch crowd, why couldn't I be open the same hours as a supermarket?

To my surprise, I got an e-mail from a *Times* editor letting me know that they would run the piece.

I was then besieged by lobbyists working on behalf of grocery chains. As a shop owner who did not dismiss the suggested changes out of hand, I was everyone's choice for the proposed law's poster boy. They were missing the point. I wasn't dying to see wine in supermarkets; I just saw an opportunity to address irrational aspects of a seventy-seven-year-old law with roots still firmly planted in Prohibition.

The more these lobbyists yearned to "work with me," the farther off the mark they got. One alternative proposal involved the creation of a medallion system like the one used for regulating New York City taxicabs. Under this plan, each current store was to be issued a medallion, which could then be sold (of course, with a transfer tax). The governor was thrilled. Not only would the state gain more revenue from the increased wine sales in grocery stores, its coffers would benefit from the fees related to the medallions.

In contrast, I saw this as a cynical attempt to pay off the small retailer who was ready to capitulate. With deep pockets and a little intimidation, the grocery chains and other large players could then buy up as many medallions as they wanted. For individual storeowners like me, the net effect would be to make expansion even more expensive. In addition to getting a lease, building out a space, and filling it with inventory, under the proposed legislation I would have to come up with an estimated $250,000 more to buy a medallion.

Fortunately, the flawed bill did not pass, thanks in part to the major distributors, such as Southern. Their motive is hardly altruistic. Rather than protecting small shop owners, the distributors are trying to maintain their profits. To them, wine in low-margin grocery stores is likely to reduce their markups while still excluding more lucrative hard liquor. With the record budget deficit, the proposed changes nonetheless remain a threat.

No matter what happened, I knew that I had to look at other ways to grow our business.

As I was standing in the checkout line at a big-box store with a shopping cart full of janitorial supplies (ah, yes, the glamorous world of wine), it hit me: Costco. Why don't we try making our own wine? Bottling our own wine certainly seemed like more fun than obsessing over economic data and outdated laws. It would be a good way to reconnect us to that journey from grape to table. Maybe we could even make a little Costco-like money.

I thought of Roland, the mild-mannered winemaker I had met several years ago at that memorable Morellino lunch at which eight Maremma winemakers had plied us with their best bottles.

"*Wie gehts?*" I asked Roland in my seriously broken German. "*Sehr gut,*" he humored me, and then thankfully slipped into an easy-gaited Italian. "Sure," he said, "we'd be open to doing something special for you." I booked tickets to Pisa for Ryan, Becky, and myself, and we were soon standing in Roland's cellars, sampling various vintages and blends. Now this was "work" we could throw ourselves into!

We wanted a food-friendly, organic Tuscan red made from native varietals. Everyone would say it was delicious, and it would cost no more than $10 per bottle. The farm already was using organic practices and was sensitive to our price limit. The only significant challenge was that the predominant native varietal, Sangiovese, can be tannic when young. Yet these grapes were hardly mouth-puckering. Roland believes it is due to the Maremman microclimate, which combines abundant sunshine with cool ocean breezes to ripen the fruit slowly. In one trip, we worked out the perfect wine. "Done!" I thought. I couldn't believe it would be so easy. Why, I wondered, don't more retailers sell their own wine?

Because it is a whopping pain to do so, I quickly discovered. The Alcoholic Beverage Control laws all but forbid the practice. According to these laws, an importer must sell to a distributor,

who then sells to us. We came upon a loophole: although a retailer cannot also be a distributor, a distributor can be an importer, in
effect eliminating one of the three tiers of the New York liquor
system. We were able to take advantage of this shortcut through
a distributor friend, Bradley Alan. Bradley was only too happy to
help, for which I owe him a debt of gratitude to this day. I pay
for everything and take care of all logistics. In return, he takes a
commission.

What I did not expect was any trouble with the label, especially given my experience with the pulp fiction illustrations that
I remembered from my tastings with Armando. If "Naked on
Roller Skates" passes muster, how hard should it be to get approval for a label inspired by eighteenth-century Luccan book-
plates?

In an effort to protect consumers, the US government requires
all imported products to go through a certificate of label approval
(COLA) process. The intent is to standardize the dizzying array
of information on wine labels. Ironically, the required information (alcohol content, origin, and the all-important government
warning) typically is crammed on the rear tag. The front label,
the one that most of us scrutinize, is primarily decorative. For
us, the stumbling block was the organic part of the certification.
In addition to proof that the grapes were organically grown, the
Alcohol and Tobacco Tax and Trade Bureau requires proof that
the vineyard uses "accepted USDA/NOP practices" (referring to
the National Organic Program) in making the wine. With our
private label, they accepted the Italian and European certification of an organic crop but not that of organic production. We
could talk to them until we were blue in the face about Roland's
reuse of gray water (wastewater from laundry, dishwashing, and

bathing), propagation of ladybugs to control flies, and husbandry of Chianina cattle (native to Tuscany and prized for their tender meat) for grazing and fertilizing, but they were not going to budge without a "recognition" agreement between the United States and Italy regarding standard organic processing. We had the spirit but not the paperwork and so were forced to write "made with organic grapes."

As frustrated as we were about the label, our ordeal underscored the difficulties with "organic" wines. With so many different accreditations and national standards (or the lack thereof), the organic designation seesaws between being unreasonably withheld and tossed around like a knee-jerk marketing adjective ("Proprietors' Reserve").

In response to the dizzying regulations and the overuse of the term *organic,* some winemakers, including ones we respect, call their wines "natural." In our experience, winemakers who eschew "organic" in favor of the lower-key "natural" tend to walk the walk—in contrast to the broader consumer product market, in which "natural" is almost meaningless. These are the owner-operators who avoid chemical fertilizers but also minimize their energy use and tend to see their farms as more than grape factories. The truth is that you do not know how committed a producer is to responsible winemaking unless you know him and have been to his vineyard. One of the most responsible producers I have met is the courtly Count Michael Goëss-Enzenberg, owner of the Tenuta Manincor in Italy's Trentino–Alto Adige region. To minimize the impact on the South Tyrolean landscape, the count's entire winery is underground. The winemaking process is gravity fed: grapes start their journey just beneath the surface and end up with wine five stories into the earth. His bottles have reusable glass stoppers. Manincor even grows his own oak for the barrels! But you will not see the "organic" label anywhere on his bottles.

Despite our semiorganic status, we decided to move ahead. I stretched our finances one last time. I emptied what was left in our bank accounts and ordered nearly eight thousand bottles.

I had shipped containers of my furniture designs from Italy before and so was at least mildly conversant with the ins and outs of boat transport. The basic ocean freight is deceptively inexpensive: $700 for a twenty-thousand-pound container. Yet I already understood that over 80 percent of the shipping cost was for charges other than the boat fare. I also knew that we wanted to ship wine in months such as May and September, when the weather is mild, to minimize the wine's exposure to temperature extremes. From distributors, I had heard horror stories of containers that had been stacked at the port in the searing sun. A few days sitting outside in a metal container could literally cook the wine.

Of course, we were going to make no such amateurish mistakes!

But on top of the label hang-up, there was a lack of urgency on the part of the trucker picking up the wine from the vineyard— the hour and a half trip took three weeks—which in turn caused another delay as the wine missed the ship and had to wait for another vessel. This is why on June 21, 2009, Father's Day, in the middle of an early summer heat wave, I found myself trembling and sweating over this wine. It was, as they say in Tuscany, a *casino* ("total mess").

I fretted over boiled wine, but I fantasized about cracking open the first bottle of our very own juice. If by some miracle the wine wasn't cooked, would it taste as good as I remembered it in Roland's cellars? The wait stirred up in me that mix of anxiety and excitement that has always been part of the appeal of opening a wine bottle. You can do research. You can know the scores. You can get advice. You may have even tasted that particular selection before. But uncorking a bottle is always a surprise. And I had thousands of bottles waiting for me on a dock in New Jersey.

Six days after it had arrived at the New Jersey port at the end of June, the container finally was delivered. After Ryan and I unloaded 660 cases by hand (no forklift), we sat down for the moment of truth. At the store, with a few bottles piled up on boxes surrounded by disarray, much as when we had first tasted with Janet, I carefully uncorked our first bottle of Pasanella & Figlio ("Son" in Italian) Rosso. I poured two tastes in our enoteca. We looked at each other for a moment. We picked up the glasses and gently swirled. The deep purply color was as I had remembered it. The nose was rich and redolent of ripe fruit. Then, for the slow slosh over the tongue:

"Wait, that's a little sharp," I said.

Ryan looked spooked. Then he took a taste and nodded in agreement.

Not good.

Determined not to panic, we let the bottle sit for a few minutes.

"Ah, yes," we both said, nodding as we took more sips. There was that familiar flavor: the tongue-caressing berryness followed by a hint of tang—just the kind of kick that would be perfect with food. It was all okay. Actually, our wine was more than okay; it was damn delicious. The only thing that remained to be seen was whether anyone else would agree.

HOMEMADE SPAGHETTI WITH LEMON ZEST

SERVES 4

In the heat of the summer, I love to make this light, refreshing pasta with a delicate sauce. To highlight the chewiness of the homemade dough, I cut it into strips that are slightly wider than spaghetti ("little strings") but not quite as wide as fettuccine ("little slices"). I suggest accompanying it with any light summer white wine, such as Vermentino, my preference. This dish also pairs well with Grüner Veltliners and Pinot Grigios.

FOR THE SPAGHETTI

2 CUPS ALL-PURPOSE FLOUR,
PLUS A FEW TABLESPOONS FOR DUSTING

2 LARGE EGGS

SALT

FOR THE SAUCE

6 TABLESPOONS EXTRA-VIRGIN OLIVE OIL

2 GARLIC CLOVES, FINELY CHOPPED

½ FRESH RED CHILI PEPPER,
SEEDS REMOVED AND FINELY CHOPPED

I LARGE LEMON, ZESTED AND JUICED

I SMALL HANDFUL CURLY PARSLEY

PARMESAN CHEESE

SALT AND PEPPER

(recipe continues)

Mound the two cups of flour on a work surface and make a hole in the middle. Crack the eggs into the hole. Beat the eggs with a fork and gently mix in the flour from the sides. Mix until the dough becomes uniform. Sprinkle more flour on the surface and start kneading the dough. If the dough is too dry or crumbly, sprinkle it with a few drops of lukewarm water.

Once the dough has been kneaded, divide it into two balls. Cover each ball with plastic wrap. Place in the refrigerator for 1 hour.

Remove one of the dough balls from the refrigerator and roll out to a rectangular shape roughly the width of your pasta maker and about ¼-inch thick. Cut away the excess. Run the rectangular dough through a pasta maker at its thickest setting. Re-feed the dough into the machine at the medium setting. Then either feed the dough into the linguini-width cutter or slice by hand to the desired width. Hang the finished spaghetti strands to dry for 1 hour. Repeat with the second dough ball.

Fill a large stock pot ¾ of the way full, and bring the water to a boil. Add a pinch of salt to ample water. While the water is heating, prepare the sauce.

FOR THE SAUCE

Heat 3 tablespoons of oil in a small saucepan over medium-high heat. After about 30 seconds, add the garlic and the chili pepper to the oil and fry lightly for 2 minutes over low heat. Remove pan from heat.

Put individual pasta bowls into the oven to warm.

Cook the pasta at a lively boil for 2 to 3 minutes (fresh pasta will cook faster than dried pasta). Drain the pasta, reserving a few tablespoons of the water, and return the pasta to the pot with the reserved water.

Pour the remaining 3 tablespoons of olive oil and the lemon juice over the cooked pasta. Add the chili-garlic mixture. Sprinkle in the lemon zest and parsley. Toss the pasta over medium-high heat for 1 to 2 minutes. Serve immediately in the warmed bowls. Grate Parmesan cheese over the pasta. Season with salt and pepper to taste.

The first bottles stacked in the store were approached warily by our customers. Like goldfish testing some new fish flakes sprinkled from above, they circled the displays and tentatively bought a few samples. Then, one by one, they started coming back. Again and again. By the time the *New York Times*'s *T Magazine* named it the "Downtown Red Wine" of the year that December, we already knew we had a hit.

chapter 7

AGE

AGING WOULD SEEM to be the most boring leg of a grape's journey from vine to table. Who wants to watch a bottle sit in a damp cellar? But in the production of some wines, the cave is a veritable ant farm of activity.

For champagne, the cellar is for riddling, a labor-intensive way to consolidate dead yeasts and other sediment before their removal. The tradition was started by the griping of Madame Nicole-Barbe Clicquot about the cloudiness of her husband's champagnes. Upon François's death in 1805, his widow (the *veuve*) took over the company and decided to solve the problem by drilling holes in her kitchen table so that she could store bottles upside down. The veuve Clicquot's idea was to let gravity push the sediment toward the bottle necks. Occasionally, she would rotate, or riddle, the bottles to shake down the residue. When the veuve was satisfied that the champagne was clear, she would remove the accumulated sediment by freezing the end of the bottle to form a plug, which she could then extract, leaving the rest of the wine intact (the *dégorgement*, or disgorging).

Instead of remodeled kitchen tables, most producers now use mechanized gyropalettes to shake and twist the bottles. A few champagne houses, such as Pol Roger, still hand riddle, a process also called *rémuage*. They store bottles neck down, at a forty-five-degree angle, in racks called *pupitres*. To riddle, a worker grabs the bottom of each bottle, shakes it, flicks it back and forth, tilts it up slightly, and then drops it back into the rack. He does this every few days for several weeks. The dregs, the lees, are then frozen and removed, just as Madame Clicquot prescribed two hundred years ago.

Yet for every champagne or first-growth Bordeaux that needs years spent underground, many—actually most— wines are meant to be drunk young. An aromatic New Zealand Sauvignon Blanc bursting with tropical fruit aromas will sag if kept for too long. A sprightly Sancerre will lose its bounce. Instead of getting deeper and richer with time, these wines just get flatter and more lifeless.

1 cs p&son, 99 john
2 cs p&son, 199 water
5 cs p&son, kasher
1 bt p&son, condé nast
10 cs p&son, boffi soho

THE DELIVERY SHEET WAS CRAMMED. Things were humming. But Ryan was bummed: "Maybe we should just forget the rest of the selections and only sell Pasanella & Figlio," he lamented. For an ex-som, I realized, much of the joy is in the hand sell, that time-consuming qualification of the cus-

tomer followed by explanations of the sommelier's recommended choices. For our peripatetic wine director, watching streams of
clients rotely scoop up the same wine day after day was disheart-
ening. More traditional retailers would be ecstatic about a wine
that sells itself. Ryan could hardly keep from moping.

I was happier than Ryan but still sweating. Three months after we had received our first shipment of our own red wine, the
first container of nearly 8,000 bottles was almost gone. We sold a
lot to event planners looking for "chic pours," as one told me. To
our surprise, customers who ordinarily would buy one under-$15
bottle at a time were now ordering cases of our wine at $10 per
bottle. Most unexpectedly, a few of our most demanding clients,
such as the surly connoisseur who only bought specially sourced
wines, were scooping up Pasanella & Figlio too. We would have
to order more. And we were back on that SLA shame list again.
We might have been done with our spending binge, but we still
had to get over our fiscal hangover. Energized by our successes, I
was determined to get us better capitalized. So I refinanced and
finally set us on firm footing.

With spring ahead, we needed to expand our private label
offering to include a white wine. Even before our first shipment
of red had arrived, Roland and I had discussed developing another wine. I wanted a Vermentino, that classic Italian summer
varietal and the perfect accompaniment to all the foods of summer. Although for me Vermentino conjured memories of seaside
lollygagging, for Roland it just meant more work. "*Zehr difficile*"
["very difficult" in hybrid German-Italian], he told me. White
wine grapes, the vintner explained, produce lower yields, the
number of bunches of grapes per vine, than do most of the varietals used in red wine. The process is also more labor-intensive

than the one used for making reds. The grapes must be kept cool in refrigerated vats to preserve what Roland calls their "fresh aromas." The fermentation is longer too, around four weeks versus ten days for reds. After fermentation, the new wine has to be recooled and held in specialized tanks.

I also was very specific about the flavor profile I was looking for. Rather than the heavier styles often produced in Tuscany and Sardinia, I preferred a cleaner, crisper sort that was more typical of what was made in cooler Ligurian climes. This meant that Roland had to be extra careful that the grapes did not overripen in the hot Maremman sun. He was game but insisted that I commit to another container.

Now, in the middle of January 2010, Becky and I returned to Italy to taste the new wine from the barrel. At that early point in its development, the cloudy juice tasted to me as much like apple cider as like wine. Yet if we were going to have the wine in New York by summer, we would have to make a decision now. Roland seemed confident that there was "nascent structure" that would ensure an elegant summer quaff. Becky and I were less convinced. Once again, it was clear, we were going to have to jump in and hope for the best. We would not be able to taste the wine again until it arrived at our doorstep in May.

Luckily, we had this lag time. As with our red wine, the label process was tricky. For wine made from the same vineyards and equipment as the previous red, the Alcohol and Tobacco Tax and Trade Bureau insisted that we revise our wording from "Made from organically grown grapes" to "Made from organically farmed grapes." I never was quite able to parse the subtle change, but I was not about to quibble with an insistent bureaucrat with the power to stall my shipment indefinitely.

After five years, we were ready to take another step toward maturity: supplying our customers with better shopping bags than our generic brown paper sacks with stickers that took eight hours a month to slap on. The quest for the perfect bag—chic, inexpensive, durable, environmentally friendly—turned out to be more difficult than making our own wine. Pretty bags are expensive and coated with nonbiodegradable sealers. Plastic-like bags made from corn were flimsy and tended to melt when exposed to liquids. I also suspected that bags made from corn produced on an industrial scale were really not that green if you took into account all that chemical runoff from those massive fields.

We started to focus on a nice reusable wine tote. Becky, Ryan, and I came up with a beauty: a custom canvas bag with leather tabs and trim, tasteful embroidery, and pockets to separate the bottles. But to break even, we would have to charge $30 apiece, plus our fancy reusable bag was made from bleached (read "bad") cotton using Chinese (read "unlikely to be adhering to Fair Trade principles") labor.

If only wine bottles weren't so heavy and so fragile.

Tyler Colman (aka Dr. Vino) pointed out that the "greatest climate impact from the wine supply chain comes from transportation . . . primarily accumulated during the final product shipment to the customer." According to wineanorak.com, if Britain switched to PET bottles for wine, the country would reduce CO_2 emissions by ninety thousand tons on this leg of transportation alone.

However, plastic lets in oxygen, which over time damages wine. There are also concerns that harmful chemicals used in plastic manufacture potentially can leach out of the material and into the wine. Needless to say, plastic also looks cheap.

The Romans preferred amphorae: two-handled clay jugs. Plentiful and inexpensive, amphorae often were broken up when they reached their destination instead of being dragged back to their points of origin. In Rome, an entire hill, Monte Testaccio, is made of these cast-off pots.

In an effort to reduce bottle consumption, one importer sells his Côtes du Rhône in mini four-liter barrels. To eliminate all those containers completely, I wish we could bring over some damigiane (the equivalent of seventy-two bottles, traditionally one month's consumption for an Italian family) and allow customers to fill their own bottles from the spigot. In Brooklyn, stores that sell beer let you fill your own growlers, sixty-four-ounce glass vessels that look like moonshine jugs. But selling wine this way is verboten in Manhattan unless you are a restaurant. Terroir, a wine bar in Tribeca, is one such place. They recently imported three thousand gallons of Riesling in a monumental bag-in-box. The sommelier fills your glass from a tap.

Despite their flaws, bottles still have their place. For ageworthy wines (albeit a very small percentage of the total wine consumed), cork-sealed bottles are best.

Not that corks are perfect. In our experience, about one in every case (approximately 8.5 percent) of conventionally sealed wine is "corked," meaning it has a spoiled flavor as a result of a loose or cruddy stopper. Think about that the next time you take a perfunctory taste at a restaurant or pop open a Soave from the fridge.

Screw caps are not necessarily better, though they're more sanitary than corks. Because screw caps allow so little air to escape, they can trap sulfur compounds, the rotten-egg-reeking preservatives found in commercial wines. The magic of a cork is that it keeps oxygen from coming in while letting the sulfur fumes out.

Even if fill-it-yourself growlers became the de facto green packaging for customers; the wine world still would have much work to do to make the trip from vineyard to store more energy efficient. From our Eastern seaboard location, for example, it is greener for us to import a wine from France by boat than from California by tractor trailer.

The perfect solution would seem to be to buy local. If only New York wines were worth it. Before you start screaming at the page, let me explain. Despite its fundamentally unfriendly wine-growing environment (too damn cold), New York makes some decent wines. They just tend to cost too much. At $20 per bottle, the shopper has a lot of choices that deliver more bangs for the buck. For example, a Loire Valley Cabernet Franc, made where this varietal has been grown for hundreds of years, generally knocks the socks off a similarly priced Long Island Cabernet Franc. New York Rieslings, vinified from a grape that seems to fare better than most varietals in cold climes, are likewise disadvantaged. From Germany, I can source whites of similar quality for 40 percent less than the Long Island versions.

Of course, there are many who would disagree with me. New York growers often complain that the large distributors, who make no money on wine that can be sold directly from local producers, freeze them out of the market. According to the New York Wine and Grape Foundation, we do not see more New York wines on the shelves of New York stores because Southern and their ilk use their muscle to keep them out.

These allegations about hardball marketing may be true, although no distributor who saw New York wines on our shelves has ever threatened me. The most intimidating thing about New York wines remains that they are too expensive, especially for products that have eliminated the importer and distributor middlemen.

In these complex circumstances, even the best intentions, such as going greener, get tricky when it comes to wine.

All of this led us back very close to where we started: a brown paper bag with a browner logo made from unbleached paper and vegetable dyes. Ryan told me that one thing was for sure: "We'll never look at bags the same way."

That year, Becky got another promotion: decorating and home editor at *Martha Stewart Living*. Good for Martha but not so good for Marco. Despite being better at tasting wine, managing employees, and discovering talent—not to mention picking paint colors—Becky was going to have to limit her role further at the shop. Instead of hearing her ideas ("How about a kids' cooking series?") or a better way to showcase our digestivi, I got e-mails titled "Becky Robertson thought you might like this item on eBay." Becky unearthed amazing stuff, such as corkscrews hidden in keys and glasses wrapped in leather, but I rued that she no longer could pop in before and after work.

It's one thing to turn one's own professional life upside down and suffer through a renovation with one's spouse. It's another to fret together about one's career, one's home, *and* the shop. So now we shared concerns about Luca's summer plans rather than about late deliveries of vermouth.

RYAN WAS BEGINNING to agonize over everything at the shop. With the smoke clear from the previous year's travails, he was prone to losing sleep about the smallest stuff.

"I'm really worried about our stapler," Ryan confided to me one day. "Are you sure our ribbon is the right width?" he brooded on another. "See the mold?" he asked, showing me the battered end of an old glue stick. "Do you think we need to check the air-conditioner filters?"

I too was having difficulty managing the transition from crisis to calm. I missed the adrenaline rush of a start-up, the back-breaking, soul-stretching process of making something from the ground up. I yearned for the thrill of schussing down an Alpine pass—on a bike. For me, 2010 became a year in which I had to learn to embrace tranquillity.

At the same time, while I chafed at the predictable rhythm of morning deliveries and evening sales, I relished that I now had the time to pop upstairs for lunch with Luca. And I did not miss for one minute watching the news at 4 a.m.

In the larger wine world, subdued grumbling had replaced outright panic. Reps were still struggling with the decline of restaurant sales. Retailers, they occasionally let slip, continued to be cautious. On one of his now infrequent visits, Armando boasted about the great success they were having in New Jersey—code, I believed, for "business in the city is still lousy." Things were eerily quiet on the big distributor front. Were Southern and Empire doing a little riddling of their own?

With Ryan's aptitude for food and wine pairings, we started a regional wine and cheese series with famed the New York cheesemonger Murray's. For each series, we picked four villages from which we sampled local products. At every tasting, we guided guests through six to eight cheeses and the same number of wines. Focusing on small areas, we found, gave us a way to explore the history and traditions of particular places, making learning about wine less intimidating and more fun. For us, the wine and cheese tastings were more comfortable than chasing down bank bigwigs for semilegal events. Bread with cheese was considered an "unassailable tidbit" according to my attorney, Stew Burg. "As long as," he added, "the cheese supplier does the slicing." With the locavore movement in full swing, the series allowed us to show that "local" means "more than from the North Fork of Long Island." For us, local is not just about geography but also about culture. And our customers were so much more engaged than in a typical Wine 101 class, where uninspired selections are washed down with stale baguettes and bricks of Brie.

In the process, Ryan the ex-musician found another way to entertain. The series were attended by so many of the same young women that John and I often teased Ryan about his groupies.

Now we just had to keep it going.

Thankfully, at the same time, another source of enthusiastic customers emerged directly across the street. The New Amsterdam Market set up shop in front of the main vacant fish market building across from which Vinnie and Carmine had stood for so many years. Once a season on a Sunday, the market set up across the street to showcase cheesemongers, artisan butchers, tea purveyors, and chocolate producers, as well as a guy who drove from Maine every time to make lobster rolls and a chef who turned spit-roasted pigs into delicious porchetta sandwiches. It was thronged. The foodies also loved their wines. Sleepy Sundays now felt more like holiday weekends.

With the sales floor in Ryan's expert hands, our enoteca became one of my favorite places to work. I often sat at a desk nestled in a corner, just within earshot but out of sight. I got a kick out of the fly-on-the-wall perspective on daily comings and goings.

A tennis ball would roll by my feet every morning around eleven o'clock. Then a wirehaired dachshund would dash in and scoop it up. Up front, the dog's master would chat with Ryan as he tossed the ball. The dachshund would dart under displays and bark at everyone who entered, but I still looked forward to the ten-minute catch sessions. I was happy to see the dog, who reminded me so much of our Guendalina, in the store.

The dachshund was not our only regular four-legged visitor. There was the bow-tied gentleman with the two pugs. The striking blonde with the majestic Great Dane. The aging hipster couple and their pair of English sheepdogs. The jock with the Lab. The German shepherd who nuzzled open the door for his laid-back master.

Dog people, it turns out, tend to be good customers. The treats we keep in a jar on the counter might help.

Sometimes the action took place right in the enoteca, oblivious to my presence.

"Honey, look at this room!" the soon to be bride exclaimed to her fiancé as she strolled into the enoteca, the back room that we originally envisioned as storage. "How about we get married here?" she asked. Over the next few months, the nervous bride called Ryan dozens of times. "Sure, we can help you with the flowers." "Try Bowne, the engravers around the corner." "Yes, we have plenty of candles." "No problem. We have room to store a walker." Honed by years of restaurant service, Ryan soothed every worry. He seemed happy having problems to tackle. The wedding went off without a hitch.

After I overheard another smitten bride, I started to fret about our accidental wedding chapel. What about the SLA? Were they going to arrest us for mixing wine with wedding vows? As usual,

Becky reassured me: "I don't think they'll put us in prison for mixing wine with wedding vows." "Besides," she added, "aren't you flattered that people come to our shop and see their future?"

We have since had sixteen unions in our tasting room, including Becky's best friend, as well as several dozen receptions and rehearsal dinners. I hope that's okay with Inspector Watts.

BACK IN ITALY, life was also settling into a more placid phase. After twenty-five years, Lisetta moved back into her own house to get more help with daily life. She now spent her days strolling around her garden, content and well tended. My father slept there every other day, but secretly felt relieved that someone could take over the responsibility for her care. Meanwhile he painted and continued to enjoy great meals and wonderful wines with good pals. He even took up smoking the occasional Cuban cigar. Hearing about his culinary adventures always got me reenthused about the store.

As the weather warmed, he was increasingly curious, as we were, about our Vermentino. Foolishly, we had changed shippers in an effort to save a little money. The new guys always answered the phone with "Marco who?" and could never tell us where our wine was in its journey. With spring just around the corner in New York, I no longer obsessed over boiling wine in Port Elizabeth, New Jersey. Instead, my gooey wine nightmares were centered on cloudless Livorno, where the wine had been taken from the vineyard. Was it now baking under the hotter Mediterranean sun while waiting for a ship to reach port? Had they parked it in a temporary storage facility? Was that place at least temperature controlled? My calls and e-mails were unanswered.

Still sitting in its steel container, the shipment appeared on the back of a semi that pulled up in front of the store ten days later. The trucker quickly unhooked the trailer and dropped it in the parking lot across the street. "You got two hours," he yelled out his window before he drove off in the cab.

Atop an even bigger and messier pile of boxes, Ryan and I repeated what was to be a ritual. This time the outcome was clear from the start: the Vermentino not only had survived the journey, it was delicious! I felt like cooking up a fritto misto, a seaside staple of fried mixed seafood, on the spot. If only I could stand.

"YOU GOTTA SEE THIS!" the thirtysomething guy yelled to his friend as he dragged him inside. "They've got a Ferrari in the store!" Then, with unvarnished childlike disappointment, "What happened to the car?"

A version of this scene happened every weekend since I sold the Ferrari two years earlier. With the business back on the rails, I thought it might be time to get another crowd-pleasing store fixture. But not another slick sports car. The world had changed. I had changed. Instead of sexy, I wanted something humble yet cheerful. In light of our increasing deliveries, I also thought the ideal car would allow us to save some money on messengers. What I found was a variation on the bare-bones Fiat on which I had first learned (and subsequently loved) to drive: a 1964 Fiat Giardiniera. Powered by a tiny 500-cc motor that produces a wheezy seventeen horsepower (but gets almost seventy miles to the gallon), the poky Giardiniera was popular with Italian nuns when I was growing up. Pale blue, with a piped red vinyl interior and a roll-up canvas roof that runs almost the length of the car, the pint-sized station wagon is also adorable. Besides, it was way easier to roll in and out of the store than the Ferrari and required no more maintenance than a lawn mower.

One trip over the Brooklyn Bridge, creeping up the ramp with my foot on the floor as cabdrivers beeped and gestured all around me, was enough to convince me that this underpowered teddy bear of a car would be more comfortable in the store, where it remains, than on the road. Our customers still fling open the doors with the same excitement but now wow their kids rather than their buddies.

Armando also seemed to be bouncing back. His new company was booming. But under the surface, there were machinations there too. One day he left another vaguely ominous message: "Call me. It's about Janet."

Again?

He gave her a promotion.

No, he made her a partner.

Yes, that's it: Crazy Janet is now going to be an unavoidable presence in the New York wine world.

Damn.

"Thanks so much for returning my call," Armando said.

"Sure," I responded.

I paused. "Here we go," I thought.

"It's about Janet," he continued.

"Uh huh," I mumbled.

"I had to . . ."

He paused.

You're killing me, Armando.

"I had to let her go."

Geez. He knew what I had told him. He had seen her in action. Now he was burned. I felt badly—at least until he asked: "By the way, got any time for me to taste you on some great new values we're bringing up from Argentina?"

You had to give him credit for relentlessness.

AS OUR FIFTH Christmas season ramped up, we noticed that the champagne business itself was experiencing underground changes. Until then, two words had been synonymous with holiday cheer: "Veuve Clicquot." There was the fresh-faced financial analyst who enunciated every syllable with her junior year abroad accent. There was the contractor with the standing five-case holiday order who asked, "You guys got my Voove yet?" Everyone seemed to equate this well-known brand with end-of-year good times. With its elegant script label, Veuve seemed less commercial than Möet. It was also less expensive that Krug and less hip-hop than Cristal. Nonetheless, in 2010, the chant for Veuve became a whisper.

Did they flock instead to inexpensive bottles of Prosecco, the Italian sparkling wine? Did they scoop up the more obscure Crémant d'Alsace, a bubbly white from the Franco-German border? Were they clamoring for Spanish cava? Not really. Granted, we still sold a lot of Prosecco and other sparklers to the more adventurous, but champagne drinkers stuck to their preferred holiday beverage. Herein lies the big deal.

Ninety-seven percent of exported champagne is made by a handful of large conglomerates (Veuve Clicquot, Mumm,

Möet, Piper-Heidsieck, Perrier-Jouët, etc.) that buy rather than grow their grapes. In recent years, these winemakers without vineyards have begun to compete with grower-producers, farmers who make their own champagne. For us, 2010 was the year that grower champagne sales overtook Veuve Clicquot and their ilk.

Grower champagnes have become startlingly popular in part because they tend to offer greater value than the name brands. For the price of a mass-produced bottle available in any duty-free shop, buyers can get a true artisan creation made of hand-sorted grapes and hand-riddled—maybe even on kitchen tables as the widow Clicquot had more than two hundred years ago. As proof of their extraordinary care, some RM (short for *récoltant manipulant*, or "grower/producer," listed on their labels) add little or no sugar to their wines. "Dosage," as it is known, can be used to mask the bitterness that comes from stems and other dross that can be swept into industrial harvesters.

Although we had been championing these artisan champagne makers, such as Egly-Ouriet and Pierre Gimonnet, for five years, Ryan and I both realized that small does not necessarily mean better. Ryan put it bluntly: "If the grapes suck, then the champagne does too."

Larger houses have the flexibility to buy from different sources to ensure a consistent style, even in weak vintages. Bollinger, for instance, favors a robust flavor that smells like hot biscuits, whereas on the other end of the spectrum, Perrier-Jouët strives for a leaner, crisper taste.

Grower champagnes bring more variation from winemaker to winemaker and year to year, making our work harder but also more rewarding. Per Se offers Pierre Gimonnet as its house champagne. In light of the fact that their sommelier was one of our customers, did they discover this gem from us? We hope so.

All in all, 2010 was shaping up to be the most happily boring year so far. We paid our bills. We expanded our selections. We solved some nagging issues. Ryan stayed out of trouble. With my Spartan drinking and enthusiastic bike riding, I dropped almost thirty pounds. Becky followed suit, eliminating her multiglass segues into postwork relaxation. Holiday sales were up 20 percent.

Then, on December 31, 2010, my dad died.

CASTAGNACCIO (CHESTNUT TORTE)

SERVES 4

A favorite of my father, this traditional Tuscan dessert has particular meaning for me. According to my father's diary, castagnaccio is the last thing he ate (along with a glass of Vin Santo, the Tuscan dessert wine) at a Christmas lunch by the lake. It's hard to believe a torte could be this good with no added sugar. Look for fresh chestnut flour (fragrant and sweet-tasting) rather than flour from chestnuts milled from the previous year's harvest. Italians are fastidious about pine nuts and contend that the best are the long and thin ones rather than the squat Asian variety.

1 1/3 CUPS FRESH CHESTNUT FLOUR

1 PINCH SEA SALT

2 TABLESPOONS EXTRA-VIRGIN OLIVE OIL

1 HANDFUL PINE NUTS (WHOLE)

Preheat the oven to 400°F. Sift the flour into a medium stockpot. Sprinkle in the salt. Slowly add 2 cups of cold water while whisking the mixture until there are no lumps. Let the dough stand for 30 minutes in the pot at room temperature.

Add 1 tablespoon of olive oil to a large cast iron frying pan. Heat on medium for 1 minute, making sure to coat the pan. Then add the flour mixture and pine nuts to the pan and smooth out. On top, sprinkle the remaining 1 tablespoon of oil. Place in the preheated oven for 30 to 40 minutes until the castagnaccio has the moist but dense consistency of a good brownie.

chapter 8

DRINK

COAXED, CODDLED, smashed, stirred, purified, bottled, labeled, and set aside. It's been a long journey from vine to table. The trip could have started on some rocky crag along Germany's Mosel River or in a verdant valley in New Zealand's Central Otago. A vineyard could have looked out over a grand seaside vista or have been nestled in a secluded glade. Once ripe, those grapes may have been plucked off by a calloused thumb or scooped up by a big machine. They could have been trampled by plump feet or thrown down a chute. Fermentation could have taken place in century-old tanks cooled by blocks of ice or in a sparkling stainless-steel lab where the juice was sprinkled with various powders and potions. The wine could have been made months ago or could have emerged after decades in a cellar. No matter what the voyage, to open the bottle is to approach the moment of truth.

Was it worth it?

———

"*I* JUST WANT YOU TO KNOW that I'm not much of a hugger," my brother said to me as we started down the ramp to the hospital mortuary. I had just gotten off the plane from New York after receiving the dreaded middle-of-the-night call. I was terrified. I expected to be led to a refrigerator drawer where an orderly would unzip a bag to let me say good-bye to my father, just as they had when my mother died on the same day a year earlier in New York.

But this was Italy. On the bottom level of the Renzo Piano–designed Italian hospital, there was a skylit room labeled "Arch. Giovanni Pasanella" reflecting respect for my dad's architect status. In the middle of the room, under a veil with "Comune di Viareggio" crocheted at the bottom, was my father, already in a white-satin-lined coffin, in one of his nice suits, wearing his beloved pair of John Lobb deerskin boots. He was cleaned up with a nice shave and combed hair, but you could tell he had not been embalmed. There was a slight discoloration around his hairline, and his jaw was slightly slack. Otherwise, he looked just like the guy who only a few days before had sent me pictures of himself and friends at a Christmas lunch by the lake in Torre del Lago.

For someone who had always told us, "When I'm gone, just spread my ashes over our *uliveto* [olive grove]," he probably would never have imagined that the hospital would have taken so much care. But laid out in such dignity, under the skylight by a famous architect, I'm sure he would have appreciated this unexpected pause on the way to the crematorium. He certainly would have been touched by the visitors: from the hospital's head of cardiology to the flowers and touching note written by our housepainter.

In one fell swoop, I lost my father, my strongest tie to the past, and my single most important inspiration for the path I have chosen. What was I doing in the vino business if not trying to capture a little of the stardust that had been his life?

The urge to turn away from Italy and the associations it conjured was stronger when we returned to the house. The place felt haunted. The Sri Lankan woman who had been taking care of my dad said as much. She told me that in the two weeks leading up to his death, she had glimpsed a shadowy black ball in his bedroom when he was out. She had even seen my father sitting in his study when she knew he was at one of his dialysis treatments. "With this eye," she said, gesturing, she had seen it all. She had confided all this to her husband in the days leading up to his death. Now she was a mess.

Ironically, our province of Lucca had been planning a retrospective of my dad's life and work for the coming summer. He was one of several creative people (the founder of the publishing house Mondadori and the art critic Cesare Garboli among them) who had found inspiration in our town of Camaiore. So I was more or less forced to start going through his things.

On his desk was the latest volume of the journal in which he had recorded thirty-five years of every meal (excluding breakfast). A full 25,550 times, he listed what he ate (funghi trifolati) and what he drank (Avvoltore '01) along with a seating chart. Overlaid onto the meals are a series of color-coded lines and shapes that I have yet to decipher. Other than the date, the menu, and the dining companions, there are no other details in his diary.

Nonetheless, for me this catalog articulated everything that inspired my journey into wine: the communion, the curiosity, the hedonism, even the obsessiveness. Was I really going to turn my back on all that?

But did I really expect to capture that magic by stocking a store full of Pinot Grigio?

The year before I opened the shop, I was asked to moderate a discussion of what it means to be Italian. Panelists included the president of Giorgio Armani, the restaurateur Mauro Maccioni, the Rome-based architect Kevin Walz, and Germano Celant, a well-regarded Italian art critic. My chief qualification seemed to have been authorship of a book called *Living in Style Without Losing Your Mind.*

After some self-congratulatory revelations about knowing how to live life well, plus a little American bashing (we are too confident in our correctness; we tend to see things in black and white), the panelists confessed that underlying all that cheerful bonhomie was pessimism. Riven by infighting and corruption, the panelists agreed, Italy is stagnant. Hopeless. The living well part is more like Nero's fiddling, a what-the-f expression of a fatalistic worldview. Being Italian, the group concluded, is not so much about cavorting in the Trevi Fountain with Anita Ekberg (the Swedish star of Fellini's *La Dolce Vita*) as about realizing that we're all going down, so at least we should enjoy ourselves along the way. Expecting cheerful nuggets of Italian sunshine and good fortune, the audience looked a little shocked.

So was I.

I've always been an uncomfortable poster boy for Italianness. Sure, I read *Diabolik* (comic mystery novels) and know every movie that Laura Antonelli ever made. I have family, friends, and a family house in Italy and even a local accent. I have an Italian passport. But I'm never going to be Italian. I am always going to be seen and, to some degree, feel like an outsider.

I'm an Italian-American. Not in the red sauce or checkered tablecloths sense. Nor in the street-smart Martin Scorsese drift. Or even in the jolly Mario Batali vein. I love the Italian culture, history, and sensuality, much of which I can savor through wine. And as a native New Yorker, I see possibilities. I believe that if you work hard, you will succeed. A rich daily life is important for many Italians, but for me it has to add up to more than an end-lessly repeated series of satisfying experiences. I want to move forward. I like to build. I guess the panelists would call me too optimistic to be truly Italian.

Since my dad passed away, I miss sharing life's little discov-eries with him. Every once in a while, I'll reach for the phone wanting to know what he ate last night. One day, excited to have met the new owner of his pal Minuccio Cappelli's vineyard, I dialed the first digit before I realized my mistake. Yet my dad's death energized me. I returned to Cannizzaro three times in 2011. With each trip, I felt more confident, more eager to em-brace the future actively.

PINK IS MY NEW FAVORITE COLOR. Six weeks after our May target, our rosé finally arrived and sold briskly. We had planned on stocking the store with our third Pasanella & Figlio wine just before Memorial Day, but more label delays pushed the delivery to end of June, effectively cutting off one-third of our summer selling season.

That we have even dared to make our own rosé reflects just how much tastes have evolved in the few years we have been in business. Previously, pink wine had been seen as enjoyable but forgettable, a pleasant by-product of summer, like salt-sprayed beach hair or a tan.

Some traditional rosés are still literally leftovers. Called *saignée,* these rosés are made from juice bled off from red wine vats to make the red wine more concentrated. In the last ten years, modern producers have gravitated toward the direct contact method in which rosé is the goal, not a by-product. These purpose-made rosés derive their pink color from limited contact with the pigment-filled skins. Considered the most prestigious, oenophiles call them *vins gris* (from the French for "gray wines"). The Italians calls them *rosati* ("pinks"). As we watched case after case move out the door, we just thought of them as bread and butter.

We'd like to think our success was due to the wine's flavor. To avoid the slightly sweet rosés that are often typical of warmer Italian climes, we harvested our Cerasuolo grapes early. As a result, our rosato was bursting with fruit but bone dry. It's possible, we imagined, that the wine's brilliant ruby color seduced our customers or that our black label beckoned "Drink me."

The quick sales even could have been due to the advance public relations work of a Seaport character, a semihomeless ex-chef with a generous imagination. "You know," he had been telling neighbors since we opened, "Marco makes an excellent blush!"

One thing was for sure: The rosé's triumph was not due to press coverage. Unlike our red wine, the rosato's debut came un-announced. I had a feeling that we had built up enough trust among our customers to let them spread the word. The *Times* writer who had raved about our Sangiovese in her review bore out my hunch: she bought a case of the rosato for herself and told us how much she loved it. Better than an official endorsement, her personal enthusiasm was valuable and much appreciated. For her, we were not just a good story; we produced wine worthy of her own house.

More than anything, rosés conjure up relaxation and beach picnics, garden lunches, and lakeside barbeques. At ten bucks a bottle, the dream came alluringly cheap.

At long last, the image of the laid-back vintner was starting to reflect the reality. From my perspective, the wine world looks better too. With the growing consumer interest (American wine consumption is up 40 percent in the last fifteen years) and ever greater sophistication of many of the producers, I see the com-ing years as very exciting for our customers. "There is now just so much good wine," I hear a lot of the reps complain, fearing the increased competition. Hard times may be ahead for winemakers as a result of continued overproduction, but wine drinkers will benefit from better wines than ever before.

Over the last five years, our customers also seem to be in a better position to take advantage of these expanded offerings. They have become both more discriminating and more adven-turous. They have flocked, for example, to the delicate wines we have carried from Aosta, the northern Italian region nestled in the Alps, and lesser known varietals such as Schioppettino, a native red varietal grown in Friuli near the Slovenian border. Leaning toward lighter, more elegant wines could be a lingering effect of the movie *Sideways* ("I'll have a [lean and elegant] Pinot Noir"), but I prefer to see it as a sign of a maturing consumer public.

In particular, I have noticed a backlash in the higher price ranges for wines that are made in an overly modern style (think big California Cabernet but from Tuscany or oaky Chardonnay but from Friuli). More and more, our customers want the real thing. They want authenticity: the wines with stories and histories, not just good branding campaigns. "Give me a Barolo that tastes like a Barolo," one of our regulars said to me the other day.

I don't want to overstate the case. Bold and expensive super-Tuscans are not dead, and people still stream in looking for a bottle of insipid Santa Margherita Pinot Grigio, the "most requested imported wine, red or white, in US restaurants," according to its importer, Terlato Wines International. But our customers seem more sophisticated than perhaps even some producers realize. Reps still overwhelm us with extra-fruity and highly alcoholic (and often very expensive) wines made for an American public whose tastes are moving on.

A customer came in and asked me: "Chardonnay's over, right?" I looked back a little dumbfounded. What did he mean? True, Chardonnay has long since been passed by Sauvignon Blanc and Grüner Veltliner as the thing to order when you sidle up to the bar. But Chardonnay, I felt like telling him, was the original noble grape. White Burgundy, arguably among the best wines in the world, is made exclusively from this storied varietal. Chardonnay, he should also know, is a very versatile grape that can be vinified (turned into wine) in many different styles. The minerally, crisp version is typical of Burgundy. The oaky, buttery iteration is more old-school Napa. By Chardonnay, did he really mean those white wines whose vanilla overtones are as overpowering as hazelnut coffees? If that's what he intended, then, yes, I would admit, tastes have changed. The heavy-handed Cali Chard has gone the way of the Hummer. Chardonnay, I wanted to tell him, is here to stay. But before I could even stammer a word, he had picked up a bottle of our Vermentino white and headed over to the register, a choice against which I could hardly argue. Next time.

From my view behind the register, not only is Chardonnay alive and well, so are a lot of other varietals too. "Thrifty Napa types," as Ryan calls them, and new wine drinkers seem to gravitate to the robust and inexpensive South American wines. Among our customers, "Malbec" seems to have become code for "California Cabernet Sauvignon at half the price."

At a wineshop that sells some liquor, one of the biggest surprises has been the rise in demand for American small-batch whiskeys. Dwarfing gin, port, rum, and vodka sales combined, high-end American whiskey now constitutes 30 percent of all our liquor sales.

One reason may be that these spirits are authentically American creations. Our whiskeys and bourbons (made of corn aged in oak barrels) have clearly identifiable house styles and stories to match. Kings County Distillery for example, bills itself as the "Brooklyn's oldest continually operating distillery since Prohibition," which, they hasten to add, means that it has been in existence since April 2010.

The New York whiskeys also owe their popularity to locaholics—customers who like to drink stuff made close by— as well as to the rise of cocktail culture. Customers clamor for a good mixed drink.

The American whiskeys also seem to have the packaging down. Tuthilltown Spirits, a popular brand made in New York's Hudson Valley, cloaks its whiskey in an irresistible petite round bottle with a wax seal. The bottle's unusually small size also conceals a premium price. Kings County plays a similar trick with its homemade-seeming hip flasks. Twenty bucks is a great price for a present; it hardly seems to matter that the 200-milliliter bottle is less than a third the size of a standard fifth (750 milliliters).

Atop the American whiskey pantheon remains Pappy van Winkle. The products of this Kentucky distillery are legendarily hard to find. When they come around, bottles tend to retail for around $200. Not that anyone quibbles about the price for this mythical bourbon. One now-defunct Brooklyn liquor store, LeNell's, owed some of its popularity to its pipeline to the Pappy Van Winkle nectar.

Another unexpected trend has been the continued popularity of Lambrusco, the dry sparkling red from Modena in Italy's Emilia-Romagna region. For years, this zesty wine was tarred with a "Riunite on ice" association. Oenophiles dismissed it as treacly fizz for those who wanted a little kick with their grape soda.

Lambrusco is a perfect foil to this region's rich and salty cheeses and charcuterie. Lay out several chunks of Parmigiano ("from Parma") with a few translucent slices of prosciutto di Parma and other salumi from Emilia-Romagna, and you would be hard-pressed not to get hooked.

HOMEMADE LIMONCELLO
YIELDS 2 STANDARD 750-MILLILITER BOTTLES

At Cannizzaro, my father always kept a treats cabinet filled with grappas and brandies, chocolates, and torrone, a sticky nougat. At the end of a meal, he loved to bring them all out and start pouring thimblefuls of all the choices. "Try this Barbaresco grappa," he would say. "How about a sip of this Dominican rum?" "Digestivo? Well," he would insist, "you should have two so that you can compare."

Lisetta first taught me to make this lemon-flavored liqueur. Becky and I love to make a few bottles at a time and give them to friends for the holidays. You can substitute blood orange for lemon peel and add a few pieces of peeled ginger root. I prefer my Limoncello more tart, as in the recipe below, but you can play with the sweetness to taste. You could also try adding bay leaf, coriander, clove, or nutmeg. I keep mine in the refrigerator so that it's handy for impulsive end-of-meal treats.

PEEL OF 10 LEMONS
(MEYER LEMONS, IF AVAILABLE)

1 750 MILLILITER (A "FIFTH")
BOTTLE OF GOOD VODKA

5 CUPS WATER

1 ¼ CUPS SUGAR

Wash and scrub the lemons. Make sure to remove any wax, coatings, or stickers. Peel the lemons into long strips and be careful to avoid the bitter white pith. Place the peels in a

(recipe continues)

half-gallon glass bottle. Pour the vodka over the peels. Seal
and store the mixture in a cool, dark place for forty days.

Once the mixture is ready, prepare a simple syrup. Stir the
water and sugar in a large saucepan over medium heat until the
sugar dissolves, about 5 minutes. Let cool. Strain the vodka
and lemon mixture (you can use a coffee filter) into a standard
wine bottle and add the cooled syrup. Serve cold.

Riesling, another much-misunderstood wine, may be poised
for a similar rediscovery. At least I hope so. Also once seen as a
synonym for cheap and sweet (think Blue Nun, widely popular
in the 1970s), this prized German varietal can be used to make
some of the best white wines. Not necessarily cloying, great Rieslings often tiptoe between unctuous and tart while incorporating
myriad other flavors. In wine-speak, they balance residual sugar
with extra acidity. Styles can range from lean to baroque, bursting with swirling aromas and flourishes of intense flavors.

During the summer of 2010 Terroir, which had brought in
a massive quantity of Riesling, chose this uncommon varietal
as its only white wine "glass pour" (wine by the glass) for the
whole summer. And Ryan is not far behind in his enthusiasm
for Riesling.

One area that has been much overlooked by my generation
is Bordeaux. Too expensive and too stodgy seems to be the general view. Who can keep track of all those growths and clas-
sifications? But I am fascinated by the original red wine ideal.
Bordeaux is true old school. It's the wine to which others owe

a debt. Bordeaux is the claret of Jefferson, the product of time-honored blends. In the 1980s, when the Italians first attempted to make their now famous super-Tuscan wines, what did they model them on? Barolos? Barbarescos? Brunellos? Bordeaux! They even planted the same varietals and used them in the traditional Gallic proportions (70 percent Cabernet Sauvignon, 15 percent Cabernet Franc, and 15 percent Merlot). I plan to rediscover this neglected superstar. I'm hoping to unearth a few values or confirm a few well-worth splurges.

At this point, with my now vast five-plus years of experience in the wine trade, I am amused by how often I'm asked about my favorite bottle of wine. During one recent lunch break, a trio of young Wall Streeters came in determined to find out.

"Wine guy, what's the best thing you've ever tasted?" asked the one with the Hermès tie. "I mean *the* best," he continued. "Gotta be a 1997 Gaja Barbaresco, right?"

"No, no, 1984 Petrus, man!" his pal interrupted, citing one of the world's most coveted Bordeaux wines in one of the worst vintages in modern history. "The guy owns the store, for chrissakes!"

The third man, the ex-quarterback busting out of his ventless suit, declared with authority: "DRC. It must have been DRC. No doubt."

None of the above. Sorry, guys.

A few months later, I was at a wine dinner in the cellar of Mario Batali's Babbo restaurant when the question was raised again.

"Prüm Wehlener Sonnenuhr Auslese 1990," opined a sommelier, taking his time to stretch out every syllable. "I can see," he said to me somewhat condescendingly, "that you are sophisticated enough to know that Riesling is the king of grapes."

"And that Prüm is a wine snob's god," I thought to myself.

"Mythic Austrian producer, wonderful vintage for this complex white, but not my Holy Grail."

From across the table, a bearded hipster suggested "Elena Walch, Beyond the Clouds, '04," referring to a rich, lush Chardonnay from a cult Italian Alto Adige producer.

Delicious and decidedly nontraditional, yes, but the best ever? I don't think so.

"If you're going Chard," countered the pale woman next to me (who looked to be about thirteen years old), "then how about a Peter Michael Belle Côte or a Kistler?" citing two of the best American whites.

"You're all missing the point," an older proprietor of a very respected wineshop jumped in. "A truly once-in-a-lifetime wine has to be a staggering bottle in an unobtainable vintage. Something like '61 Petrus," he said, referring to the world's most famous Merlot in one of the best postwar years.

All great wines, but none are my favorites.

Not surprisingly, for me, the answer starts in Italy. As a boy, I used to race bicycles for the G.S. Versilia (Gruppo Sportivo Versilia) team in races around Tuscany and Liguria. My bedroom was plastered with posters of my idols, Eddy Merckx, the Belgian champion nicknamed the Cannibal, and Francesco Moser, Italy's 1970s superstar cyclist. I dreamed of winning the Giro d'Italia and the Tour de France.

The competitions were grueling fifty-milers often ending with steep climbs up Appenine peaks. In one race, I remember finishing atop the Passo della Cisa, which runs up through Pontremoli toward Parma. As we neared the summit of the ten-mile ascent, our breakaway (a small group ahead of the main bunch of 100 or more racers) pedaled through a wet fog. My legs throbbed. My lungs burned. I was bleary-eyed and at my limit. In the distance, I could barely make out a stooped figure draped in scarlet silk and standing among the clouds: a cardinal. As we neared the summit, I gave it one last push, only to find my archrival, Mauro Cima from the Del Tongo shoe team, whiz by me as we passed the finish line, where His Excellency nonetheless blessed us both. Thankfully, what awaited us was not the pearly gates but, in my case, a small prosciutto, a pair of women's slippers (for Mamma), and a *fiasco* (the old-fashioned straw-covered bottle) of Chianti as my prizes. That night, over a dinner of I can't remember what, our family cracked open the flask. It was and remains the best-tasting bottle of wine I have ever had.

But that doesn't mean that I won't keep trying to top that hard-earned fiasco.

I WANT TO ORGANIZE a bike ride in our new Pasanella & Son bike jerseys and come back to the store to slake our thirsts. We have many plans for the coming years.

We want to have a summer festival for the community. Ryan calls it "Pasanella-palooza." We're imagining sabrage demonstrations in which we chop off champagne bottle tops with sabers as they did in Napoleon's time and Catalan men pouring Txakoli from behind their heads (the traditional method of aerating this aromatic white wine). Maybe there'll be a cookie tasting for kids (along with something a little stronger for their parents). I'm partial to recreating the feelings of some festivals of my youth at which we ate and drank one thing (e.g., lardo, the delicious fatback aged in the nearby marble quarries, washed down with Colli di Luna, the refreshing white wine grown on the slopes just below those quarries) on long benches. The Lees, our store band, are due for a comeback, at least for a day.

We've now had the store for six years, the same span Jefferson spent in France (1784–1790) indulging in months-long vineyard trips. His next act was to return to the States to become secretary of state. Mine? Becky thinks I should run for local office. I think she is blinded by love.

We've been toying again with the idea of opening another location. Flower district? West SoHo?

For all the boyfriends who stand dutifully by their girlfriends as they pick up bottles of rosé, we've been weighing opening an artisan beer shop next door. Or we could open a florist, a bike shop, or even a candy store.

And might it be fun to introduce some great small-producer American wines to Italy?

IT'S MONDAY, a little before seven o'clock. Shuffling half asleep into our living room, I see the city already in motion. The Brooklyn Bridge glints in the morning sun. Across the harbor, car headlights move along the Brooklyn-Queens Expressway like a news ticker. Five-story-high freighters float by at eye level as they cruise up the East River. If I'm feeling inspired, I may jump on my bike and head uptown for a few laps around Central Park. If not, I'll get the coffee going, make Luca's lunch, and lay out his clothes while he and Becky sleep. In a few minutes, Becky will scream, "I'm so late," and hustle Luca out the door to school. I'll wave out the window as they jump unaware into a cab.

In a few minutes, I'll head downstairs, cappuccino in hand, and hang out our gold-leafed bottle on the hook that the fishmongers used for their scales. Ryan and I will chat. We'll do a little paperwork. Deliveries will arrive via chatty truckers. The wirehaired dachshund will drop by. Then there'll be the lunch flurry of nearby office workers. After that I'll probably pop upstairs to make myself a quick lunch. In the afternoon, a fledgling rep may drop by trawling a wheelie bag. Usually we turn them away if they don't have an appointment, but if the store is quiet, we may taste. Around three-thirty, Luca will come running in from school and hug me as if he hasn't seen me for years. Then, just as quickly, he'll bound up the stairs, barely managing "Bye." Starting in the late afternoon through closing at 9 p.m., there'll be a steady stream of regulars. From my hidden perch facing our ivy-covered garden, I'll listen to Ryan wax over some great new Spanish find or rattle off a series of perfect pairings. I'll often catch women giggling. Customers, now friends, will ask, "Is Marco around?" I'll peek out, end up chatting, and lose track of time. Dinner will be late. I'll race upstairs carrying a half-empty sample bottle. We'll nibble as I cook—so much for laid-back European dinners. At the end of the day, I'll head downstairs one last time, take down the gold bottle, and pull down the store gates.

Every once in a while, I'll peek in the darkened store windows from the street. I'll pause over the glistening bottles in the lighted cabinets, the stacks of wine neatly arranged on the floor, the mosaic tile "Pasanella & Son" that looks like it's been there forever, the little Fiat poised for action. I'll look at all of it lying in suspended animation, and I will thank my stars that I have been so lucky as to have Becky and Luca, to have tripped over this building, to have a business that is also my passion, to have found someone as knowledgeable and committed as Ryan, to have changed my life.

This is not to say that no frustrations persist. There's the relentlessness of the dolce vita. The business of providing a good time can be exhausting. After six years helping customers celebrate, I sometimes need breaks from the party. I also realize that making and selling wine is as cyclical as designing and redesigning apartments. And nine years after my initial purchase, we are just now—finally!—finishing the building renovation.

Yet these irritations pale in comparison to the satisfaction. I'm less manic about keeping up with wine minutiae, about mastering every obscure varietal in Jurançon Sec (an appellation in France's far southwest). I'm more focused on who comes in the door, more content with communion and good experiences than wanting an encyclopedic knowledge of the latest scores. One of the most valuable lessons I learned from John, who has been cheerful every single time he's worked at the store since 2006, is that the secret to a great wineshop is not chasing the newest fads and hippest producers; it's being knowledgeable and friendly. It's about building trust between you and your customers so that they'll take your word that the risky liquid in that dark bottle is worth the expense.

More and more, I find myself asking, "What about Luca?" What legacy do I want to leave the "Son"? Cool neighborhood shop? Venerated brand? Dad's crazy midlife experiment?

In the end, I'm not sure it really matters whether he knows his Gattinara, a robust Piedmontese red, from his Amarone, a robust Venetian red. If I can give Luca one gift, passed down from his grandfather to me, it's to value a life filled with discovery and possibility. I hope that Luca will, as I remain, always be looking for the next bottle to open.

APPENDIX

THE FIVE BIGGEST MISCONCEPTIONS ABOUT WINE

WINES ARE PRICEY and rarely tasted before purchase, and wine shopping often is based on rumor and speculation. It's no wonder that some surefire theories are as rational as bloodletting.

There are many more wine wives' tales (e.g., "all sparkling wine is champagne," "Bordeaux is a grape," "Rieslings are sweet"), but here are some of the biggest misnomers.

1. NINETY POINTS MEANS I'LL LIKE IT. A high rating just means that someone, who may or may not have this vineyard as a major advertiser, likes it. A 90-point wine is unlikely to be crummy, but that's setting the bar a little low. It's better to experiment with a few inexpensive bottles and find what you enjoy. Armed with your preferences, a good wine merchant should be able to give you excellent suggestions.

2. ALL WINE SHOULD BE STORED ON ITS SIDE. Common wisdom is that wine benefits from the cork maintaining contact with the liquid it is there to protect. The wine prevents the cork from drying out and therefore prevents damaging air from slipping in. More recent studies point to the benefits of keeping

wine at a slight angle, allowing the cork to sit against enough wine to keep it moist, but with enough air to allow the bottle to breathe. According to both the Oxford Companion to Wine and the Comité Interprofessionel du Vin de Champagne (CIVC), champagne should be stored upright as moist contact with the wine can damage a cork's elasticity, thereby letting in damaging oxygen.

3. THE MORE EXPENSIVE THE WINE, THE BETTER IT IS. You would think we all would know better. This is not true, but some vineyards deliberately play on this insecurity by jacking up their prices to imply higher quality. This practice so irks our wine director that he sometimes will go to great lengths to dissuade a buyer from selecting what he considers to be an overpriced wine. This is not exactly what an owner wants to overhear, but you have to admire his integrity.

4. IT'S GOING TO GIVE ME A HEADACHE. People get headaches from wine for two reasons: they are sensitive to sulfites, the naturally occurring by-product of winemaking that often is added as a preservative, or they drink too much. All wines have some sulfites, but white wines generally have less than do reds. Natural and organic wines typically are made with the lowest amount of added sulfites possible. To avoid headaches, try a natural white. Or refrain from emptying that bottle!

5. RED WINE IS MORE SERIOUS THAN WHITE. Nor does the color of your beverage need to be related to your gender. Both observations are just steakhouse myths. Try a glass of Chateau d'Yquem, the honey-colored French Sauterne, which is one of the most coveted and expensive wines in the world. Or take a sip of Bâtard Montrachet. Or crack open a Riesling from Germany's Saar Valley. You will discover that red wine is no more worthy of veneration over white wine than are red cars over white ones.

THE TEN STRANGEST WORDS IN WINE

PEOPLE IN THE WINE BUSINESS talk in a shorthand that's intended to communicate an experience by using a universal language. Ironically, the result can be almost inscrutable to the outsider. "Notes of Oriental saddle leather?" "Black fruit?" Here's how to parse the code:

1. CAT'S PISS: The desirable smell of some Sauvignon Blancs. A compliment used by nerds to be racy. "Boxwood" is used as a more polite synonym for this aroma.

2. CHEWY: A wine so full-bodied that you could gnaw on it. Another compliment.

3. CORKED: The unpleasant musty flavor from a cork fungus. It basically means that the wine is junk.

4. DIRTY SOCKS: Usually a bad thing, except in moderation in a few very exquisite French Burgundies, in which the term is meant to invoke the pleasing aroma of decay that arises from a wet forest floor rather than the stink of old running shoes.

5. FLABBY: A derisive term that refers to a wine without sufficient acidity.

6. FRUIT BOMB: A wine that tastes overwhelmingly like grapes. It can be appealing, but it's considered unrefined.

7. **FUNKY**: Smells like rotting organic material, such as a wet log. It can be good or bad. Serious collectors tend to like some funk in their wines (see "Dirty socks," above).

8. **HOT**: A wine that burns your tongue with too much alcohol.

9. **RISING BREAD DOUGH**: A yeasty smell often found in champagnes. It's considered somewhat negative unless you call it "biscuity" or "toasty," which means the same thing but sounds better.

10. **PETROL**: The gasoline-like attribute of some very vaunted German Rieslings. Although it sounds disgusting, a petrol or diesel nose is a desirable trait.

FIVE TIPS ON TASTING WINE

I STARTED OUT WINE BLIND. I read a lot. I memorized vintage tables. I knew what was supposed to be good. I could even tell you what was cool, but I didn't really know how to taste. Here are a few of the most important things I learned:

1. **YOU HAVE TO GET A LITTLE TIPSY.** We taste sixty to seventy wines in our weekly appointments with distributors, and nothing I ever read has taught me more. I spit (at least when it's not a vintage Barolo), but I still feel slightly woozy after a couple of hours.

2. **SKIP THE COFFEE.** That cup of joe will kill your palate for a good half hour.

3. **FORGET THE "LEGS."** Earnest wine tasters study the drips on the inside of the glass as if reading tea leaves. Pros look at the color of a wine for various things—hints that it may have been chemically altered, signs that it may be past its prime—but no one really cares about the dribbles.

4. **LEAVE THE GARGLING FOR MOUTHWASH.** Neophytes often make a big production out of swishing wine around their mouths. But what you really want is just a gentle swirl, enough so that those aromas can reach the back of your nose.

5. **SNIFF THE CORK TO SEE IF THE WINE IS BAD, NOT TO REACH ORGASM.** Deep inhalation and fondling of the wine's stopper is another newbie tip-off.

TEN WAYS TO TASTE WITHOUT FEELING LIKE A SNOB

1. **PULL OUT.** Check a bottle for obvious suspicious signs: Is the label unmarked? Is the capsule (the metal cover that encloses the cork) in good condition? Beat-up bottles can reflect a history of equally rough storage. When you remove the capsule, check to see that there are no obvious red flags here too, such as moldy or protruding corks.

2. **POP.** Take a look at the cork. Does it look okay (not crumbling or green)? Does it smell okay (no funky odors)? If it's an expensive bottle, does the name on the cork match the one on the bottle? Skip enthusiastic fondling and dramatic resniffing of said cork. That just makes you look like a pretentious nitwit.

3. LEAVE OPEN. Most wines get better when exposed to a little air, so leave the bottle open for up to twenty minutes before serving. Red wines, particularly old ones, like to be decanted. This allows the wine to be aerated and any sediment to be removed. Whatever you decant will need to be drunk that day. Only in the rarest situations is a wine actually better the next day.

4. POUR. For maximum aeration, fill to the widest part of the glass (less if you are not going to drink it).

5. LOOK. There are some people who can't help but marvel at the colors of wines as if they were pondering a Monet water lily. I am not one of them. I take note (light red, golden yellow, etc.) but generally I am looking for something suspicious, such as a brown cast that could indicate that the wine is past its prime or has been exposed to heat. I don't go crazy admiring a wine's color and limit my ogling to my wife.

6. SWIRL. This part is tricky to do without looking silly. A flick of the wrist does indeed help bring out the most in a wine by further aerating it as well as encouraging the aromas to waft up the glass. However, avoid ostentatious whirling and vigorous shaking. You want to open up the wine's bouquet gently. In the Northern Hemisphere, you can choose to swirl counterclockwise (the opposite direction that water naturally goes down a drain) for maximum effect. Just don't draw attention to it.

7. SNIFF. With the bottle open, most of us are tempted to dive right in. Pause. Smelling a wine does not have to be snooty. Linger over the aroma not because you are acting like a wine aficionado but because you want to savor something enjoyable. To skip smelling a wine is to deprive oneself of part of the visceral reward of drinking it.

8. **SIP.** Some pros swear by a sucking method by which the wine is practically vaporized before it goes down your throat. Almost like whistling in reverse, this dramatic technique is effective but is overkill in most situations. An unhurried swish followed by a gentle pass over the tongue is all you need to really taste a wine. The key here is to breathe, as so much of a wine's taste is in the smell. Just avoid the bottoms-up gulps you practiced with shots of spring break tequila. And if you taste more than a few bottles at a time, don't forget to spit!

9. **INVITE.** Tasting is always more fun when shared. I love tasting wines with friends, even if we disagree.

10. **REPEAT.** Let blowhards make ceremonial fusses at important business dinners and wedding receptions over napkin-wrapped bottles of expensive wines. Instead, seek out regular enjoyment of the thousands of truly enjoyable wines under $20. In a few months, you will know more than they ever will about good wine.

TEN OF MY FAVORITE WINE AND FOOD PAIRINGS

HERE'S MY DREAM TEAM of wine and food combinations. Some echo each other's tastes; others are complementary, making both food and wine better than they would have been without each other.

1. **MOSCATO AND LEMON RISOTTO:** Dry, aromatic white meets zesty rice for a refreshing hookup.

2. **RIESLING AND SEA SALT-CRUSTED MUSSELS:** Sweet offsets salt, and you don't have to be a wine geek to find yourself oohing.

3. **LAMBRUSCO AND SALUMI:** This tart and sparkling red is just the thing to cut the richness of prosciutto and Parmigiano. It's a classic combination but one worth remembering in light of Lambrusco's lingering and outdated reputation as gooey 1970s fizz. Good Lambrusco is also ideal with Mexican food and barbeque.

4. **CHIANTI CLASSICO AND RIBOLITTA:** A classic combination that's a textbook case for figuring out how food can enhance wine. Chianti's rich flavors are highlighted by this tomato-y white bean stew, which also drowns out its harsher tannins.

5. **MEURSAULT AND MORELS:** Pair smoky whites with blanquettes de veau, a French veal stew, smothered with creamy morels for love on a mossy forest floor.

6. **CHINON AND SALMON:** A chilled, light red (yes, red) tames this rich fish.

7. **PINEAU DE CHARENTES AND ALMONDS:** A slightly sweet brandy mixed with grape juice is not wine but is just the thing for almonds, especially with almond pound cake or tangy amaretti (almond cookies).

8. **CHAMPAGNE AND POPCORN:** Crisp bubbly meets hot buttered popcorn for the best high-low combination since Katherine Hepburn and Spencer Tracy.

9. **BEAUJOLAIS AND ROAST CHICKEN:** The secret to this simple combo is in the quality of both the food and the wine. Splurge on a cru Beaujolais, a graceful wine that won't overwhelm the

bird. And get the best Bresse chicken, roasted in a lemony sea salt crust.

10. **BAROLO AND TRUFFLES**: Food and wine from the same place, Piedmont's Asti in this case, often make perfect pairings. Gamy aged Barolo is tailor-made for matching with a few shavings of these musky, earthy mushrooms over pasta fresca (freshly made egg noodles).

TOASTS

THE BABY IS BORN. The groom is married. The deal is done (and the boss is watching). It's a very special moment. And you are . . . speechless. Here's a cheat sheet for the perfect sentiment.

ANNIVERSARIES

Here's to you both,
A perfect pair,
On the anniversary of your
    love affair.
You're not as young as you
    used to be
But you're not as old as you're
    going to be
So watch it!

—IRISH PROVERB

BABIES & KIDS

We haven't all the good fortune to be ladies; we have not all been generals, or poets or statesmen; but when the toast works down to the babies we stand on common ground. We've all been babies.

—MARK TWAIN

A baby will make love stronger, days shorter, nights longer, bankroll smaller, home happier, clothes shabbier, the past forgotten, and the future worth living for.

BIRTHDAYS

Time marches on!
Now tell the truth—Where
   did you find
The fountain of youth?
Another candle on your cake?
Well, that's no cause to pout.
Be glad that you have strength
   enough
To blow the damn thing out.

BUSINESS

In matters of style, swim with
the current. In matters of
principle, stand like a rock.

—THOMAS JEFFERSON

Here's what my lawyer taught
   me—
Say it with flowers,
Say it with eats,
Say it with kisses,
Say it with sweets,
Say it with jewelry,
Say it with drink,
But be careful, never, never say
   it with ink.

FOR ANY OCCASION

Here's to you with a glass full
   of bubbles
To blow away all your troubles.

Three be the things I shall
   never attain,
Envy, content, and sufficient
   champagne!

—DOROTHY PARKER

HEALTH

To your good health, old
friend, may you live for a
thousand years, and I be there
to count them.

—ROBERT SMITH SURTEES

Here's to your health,
You make age curious, time
   furious
And all of us envious.

HOLIDAYS

Be at war with your vices, at
peace with your neighbors,
and let every year find you a
better man.

—BENJAMIN FRANKLIN

May all your troubles during
   the coming year be as
   short as your New Year's
   resolutions.
I have known many,
Liked not a few,
Loved only one,
Here's to you!

Here's to those who'd love us,
If we only cared;
Here's to those we'd love,
If we only dared;
Here's to one and only one,
And may that one be he
Who loves but one and only
  one,
And may that one be me.

WEDDINGS

Here's to the health of the
  happy pair,
May good luck meet them
  everywhere,
And may each day of wedded
  bliss,
Be always as sweet as this.
May your wedding night be
  like a kitchen table,
Four legs and no drawers!

—IRISH SAYING

A NOTE ON WEDDING TOASTS

Toasts are offered once all the guests have been seated and have been served their drinks. At less formal gatherings, toasts should be offered after everyone has gone through the receiving line and been served a drink. At a large wedding, it may be more practical to do most of the toasting at the rehearsal dinner rather than at the wedding reception. In either case, toasts generally are offered to the bride and groom, beginning with the best man. The groom then responds with a toast of thanks. Other toasts may follow in this order: fathers, beginning with the father of the bride; mothers, beginning with the mother of the bride; groom to the bride; bride to the groom.

TOASTING TIPS

Offer a toast to the guest of honor only after the host has had the opportunity to do so.

Never toast when you are drunker than your fellow guests. What you find hilarious may be offensive to the less inebriated.

Be yourself and be sincere. Chances are, your dinner partners either know you and like you or want to.

Fill your glass with anything other than water, at least according to my superstitious Italian stepmother. Pause to let the others refill their glasses.

Stand up, but don't bang a spoon on your glass unless you're a teenager or want to risk shattering someone's good crystal. The toastee should remain seated.

Introduce yourself and speak slowly, clearly, and as loudly as if you were talking to your hard-of-hearing grandmother.

Hold your glass in your right hand when proposing the toast and raise the glass toward the person you are toasting when you are finished. Europeans expect to be looked in the eye as a sign of your sincerity. At small tables, clink every glass after the toast. To avoid bad luck, be careful not to cross arms with another person.

Conclude by raising your glass and saying "Cheers!" (see page 211 for how to say "Cheers!" in many languages).

If you choose to wing it, remember:

Humor is good, humiliation is not. Keep the toast clean and appropriate, avoiding inside jokes and potentially embarrassing sentiments.

The toast should be no more than a minute or two. It's a toast, not an Oscar speech, and it's not about you.

CHEERS! (IN TWENTY-
SEVEN LANGUAGES IN
ALPHABETICAL ORDER)

Arabic: Shereve! Hanya
  Bismallah!
Armenian: Genatsoot!
Basque: Osasuna!
Cantonese: Gom bui!
Czech: Na zdraví!
Danish: Skål!
Estonian: Terviseks!
French: Santé!
German: Prost!
Hebrew: L'Chayim!
Italian: Salute!
Japanese: Kanpai!
Korean: Guhn-bae!

Latin: Sanitas bona!
Nigerian: Mogba!
Oriya: Chitta!
Portuguese: Saúde!
Quechua:
  Ukyaykusun!
Russian:
  Vashe zdorovie!
Spanish: Salud!
Thai: Chokdee!
Ukranian: Bud'mo!
Vietnamese: Chúc mung!
Welsh: Lechyd da!
Xhosa: Impilo!
Yiddish: Mazel tov!
Zulu: Oogy wawa

ACKNOWLEDGMENTS

I BELIEVE THAT THANKS are a lot like toasts: Be brief, be direct, and tell the truth. So here goes:

I thank my agent, David Kuhn, whose idea it was to write this book (as well as his wise and cheerful colleagues Jessi Cimafonte and Billy Strickland). I thank Doris Cooper and Lauren Shakely at Clarkson Potter for believing Mr. Kuhn. Even greater thanks go to my editor, Emily Takoudes, for her unerringly sage counsel and apparently limitless patience. Thanks too to Emily's assistant, Hilary Sims.

I'd also like to express my gratitude to my friends Enrico Bonetti and Francesca Forcella, who selflessly collaborated on much of the "research" required for a book on drinking wine; thanks too to Tom Molner and Andy Brimmer, who have also been sassy and enthusiastic volunteers. *Grazie* as well to Fabio Ercolini and Sabrina Puccetti, with whom I have treasured friendships lubricated by good food and wine. David Shipley deserves thanks for encouraging me to write (after recusing himself) the op-ed piece on New York's crazy wine laws, which came to the attention of David Kuhn. Thanks (and love) also to Jodie Foster, who continues to show me how to be fearless even when terrified. Huge and bottomless gratitude to my pal Will Schwalbe, who, in addition to being the smartest man I know, is modest, encouraging, and, above all, a true and cherished friend. My thanks also to David Cheng, Will's partner, who has patiently sat through more chatter about this project than anyone deserves.

There could be no book on wine without winemakers. I would like to thank all whom I have mentioned in these pages (Fabio Burlotto; Laura Collobiano and her oenologist, Saverio Petrilli; Luca D'Attoma; Alessandro Mori; Stephane and Mireille Tissot) as well as many others who continue to inspire me with their dedication. I would like to extend a special thanks to our winemaker, Roland Krebser, as well as to Klaus Egger and Elodie. Also worthy of appreciation are the importers, distributors, and sales reps driven by similar passion. In particular, I wish to acknowledge Bradley Alan, Guglielmo Mattiello, and Neal Rosenthal.

A store is only as good as the people who work there, and with few exceptions, we have been blessed. I'd like to thank all the people who work and have worked here, especially Suzanne Zudiker, John Lahart, and, of course, Ryan Ibsen. Similarly, there would be no store without customers and neighbors, so a big *grazie* to all of them. Also included in my thoughts are our former neighbors, the fish merchants, especially Vinnie and Frank Fogliano, who embraced a stranger in their midst with open arms.

My greatest thanks go to my family: to my father, my mother, my brother, and Lisetta, without whom I never would have discovered the connection between wine and my dreams. Above all, I want to express my love and gratitude to my wife, Becky, who makes me feel like a better version of myself and with whom I share the greatest joy in my life, our son Luca.